What Others Are Saying About

D1541318

"Does your company know the rules, of playing business-to-business golf. Here's one: Take Mike's book back to ...

– Thomas W. Wade, President
Wade Associates

"No matter how much—or little—experience you have playing golf, by reading this book you can learn important lessons that will increase your chances of business success."

– Judith Hoffman, President
JCH Enterprises

"A useful guide on how to combine golf and business and entertain customers on the golf course."

– Ray John Campbell, Corporate
Import/Export Manager, BIC Corporation

"This book makes it easy for everyone, from weekend duffers to seasoned pros, to understand the parallels between the golf course and business markets. A painless way to get your feet wet in today's economy, using golf as a jumping-off point."

– Robert J. Becker, Chief of Staff
Congressman Benjamin A. Gilman

"There is nothing out there like this book! Very helpful and informative. Great way to help you learn how to play business-to-business golf with your customers and get new business!"

– Roland Irby, Business Development Manager
Zachry Construction Corp.

"Business-to-business golf is becoming a common practice. When done right, it's very effective. Many articles have been written on the topic, but nothing as clear, concise and comprehensive as this."

– John A. D'Ambrosio, Ed. D.

"This is an informative, resourceful and pleasurable way to help you with business and with how to swing your way to business success on the golf course."

– Robert Minicozzi
Metropolitan PGA golf professional

BUSINESS-TO-BUSINESS
GOLF

How to Swing Your Way
to Business Success

MICHAEL ANDREW SMITH

InfoPro Publishing ■ New Windsor, New York

Business-to-Business Golf: How to Swing Your Way to Business
Success © 2000, 2002, 2005, 2010 by Michael Andrew Smith

InfoPro Publishing
PO Box 4201
New Windsor NY 12553-0201

www.business2businessgolf.com
businesstobusinessgolf.com

Fourth edition
Printed in the United States of America
Book design by Sara Patton

Publisher's Cataloging-in-Publication
(provided by Quality Books, Inc.)

Smith, Michael Andrew.
    Business-to-business golf : how to swing your way to
business success / Michael Andrew Smith. -- 1st ed.
    p. cm.
    Includes bibliographical references and index.
    ISBN: 0-9703662-0-5
    ISBN13:978-0-9703662-0-7
    1. Success in business. 2. Business entertaining.
3. Golf--Psychological aspects. 4. Public relations.
5. Strategic planning.   I. Title.

HF5386.S65 2000   658.4'095
                             QBI00-783

CONTENTS

APPENDIX

ACKNOWLEDGMENTS

I wish to thank my loving wife, Ann, and our two children, Laura and Michael, for their understanding and support of this project. Their love and encouragement during many grueling hours of re-writes, discussion of opinions and research helped me to accomplish a dream of writing this book. I dedicate this work to you. Thank you so much.

It is especially important to recognize others who have also helped greatly with this work:

- Edison Guzman, who has kept this publication a challenge with the needed direction,

- Anna Morabito Tilley for keeping the thought process in check and giving added homework assignments,

- Judy Hoffman for her watchful eye and careful analysis,

- Nancy Proyect for keeping the words flow just right,

- Kathi Dunn and Mary Jo Jirik for their artistic cover design talents,

- Sara Patton for interior design and layout,

- Susan Kendrick and Graham Van Dixhorn for the special cover wording,

- Cheri Hoffman for her constructive review,

- John Long for his printing acumen,

- The Smith family—my mother, brother and my father.

To all of you, thank you very much.

INTRODUCTION

Golf and business have strong links to one another. Each can be fun, certainly competitive, and there is a never-ending thirst for knowledge and ways to improve both.

I was twelve years old when I first picked up a club. I took several lessons and played and played and played. I was fortunate enough to play on high school and college golf teams. After my school days, competition in many amateur tournaments helped keep my interest in the game. It took a while, but I came to understand that golf is truly a lifetime sport. It is addictive, time-consuming, competitive, and requires establishing relationships — quite a lot like business.

This was similar to how I learned my professions — through many hours of education and endless experience. I spent eight years in the financial services industry (mostly insurance and banking), followed by becoming a partner in a manufacturing business for twenty years, and my present work as a business development engineer and consultant. These experiences have involved me in many different kinds of business situations with customers. Each one has taught me a lesson.

1

Many businesses invite clients, prospective customers, or people they may hire, to play golf. A lot of business can happen on the golf course, but golf also has a way of bringing out the best and sometimes the worst in a person's character. Favorable or unfavorable impressions may be developed after playing just a few holes. For my first business-to-business golf experience, during my insurance selling days, I invited a client to my golf club with the hope of solidifying and developing a long term business association. At first, I felt that I had to be polite, even diplomatic, and not play my best (since I happened to have a single-digit handicap). For some reason, I did not want to beat my guest even after factoring handicaps. So I faked it a little. But every now and then the guest would ask if I were giving the game my full effort. I finally realized it was okay to play my normal game. If I happened to play a better round than my guest, it would not ruin any business relationship.

This realization was a relief, particularly since my game was getting a bit sloppy. From then on, I decided to focus on my game, drop my salesperson mode, and just make sure my guest was having a good time. If I happened to be asked for a golf tip, I gave it my best effort. If the player was a better golfer, I asked for help. But most of all, it was important just to relax and enjoy the round of golf together.

I always look forward to a round of golf. I have enjoyed it so much that I have volunteered on various golf committees that run tournaments and events, including a junior golf program. For me, golf has become a blend of personal satisfaction, a release from business stress and pressures, and a way of developing friendships with different types of people, some of whom may become clients. I think of it as *golfship*.

A lot of different topics may be talked about during a business-to-business golf round. It does not matter if the person you are entertaining is a client or a prospective client, or if he or she plays golf only occasionally or is a serious player. The goal is to be sure you understand your role while playing business-to-business golf. What should be said or not said? What is the appropriate etiquette in given situations? How much does one need to know about golf rules? How does one prepare for a round of business-to-business golf? What are some business topics that may be discussed? How can you improve your business and your chances of closing a deal by playing business-to-business golf?

Many companies invest significant dollars to join golf clubs, primarily for business-to-business golf purposes. However, too many business owners, managers, sales people, decision-makers, account executives, business developers and the like may overlook or neglect making the effort to learn and understand the appropriate behaviors for business-to-business golf. If you know your field of work, feel good about what you do, and attempt to know and understand the person you are conducting business with, there is unlimited potential. But it is equally important not to try to impress your invited guest with your knowledge or press for a sale! Be patient and listen to what the person is saying and ask questions. You may be able to develop a good, lasting relationship that may yield many sales, and have some fun while doing it.

By learning and understanding the business-to-business golf principles, etiquette and rules, you will be able to help yourself play at peak levels and quite possibly close a deal or open a new relationship. This is the most desirable outcome. But it takes time, patience and practice. There are many steps to be taken. The eighteen chapters that follow are designed to help you maximize your success on the golf links. But that's not all.

Business people are involved with many different issues and wear many hats. One never knows what may be discussed in business-to-business golf. Of the many business issues, eighteen have been selected for this edition. The chapters are not intended to be long dissertations or to teach each subject in complete detail. They are intended to be thought-provoking and help you. They are to be used as a stimulus for action. Take an idea and run with it! By doing this, you should not only create more free and creative time but be able to entertain customers and prospects more often and effectively and sharpen up your game, too.

These pages are personal reflections on my business and golf experiences and a description of how they team up as an exciting pair. Let's get started. Let's see how you can swing your way to business success. Enjoy your round of business-to-business golf!

ach of the following eighteen chapters begins with a golf hole, followed by a given business-to-business golf situation. You then have an opportunity to play the hole and give yourself a score. There is a scorecard at the end of the last chapter to record all chapter scores (page 112).

Immediately following your score, there is a section on a related business theme that is tied into the chapter heading. The tips that follow are designed to provide you with information on the selected business topic and to be a resource for ideas that may help you with your work so that you can create more free time to play business-to-business golf.

As you play this round of golf, hole by hole, chapter by chapter, be sure to score yourself honestly and accurately. Make note of the business information resources along the way. The goal is to help you with your business-to-business golf play and provide good tips for your business.

PURSUING A DREAM
Focusing on the Big Picture

1ˢᵗ HOLE: It took a major effort, but you have finally achieved your dream of having your most important client accept an invitation to play. Play begins. Both you and your guest start with good drives off the first tee. For your third stroke, you have a short pitch shot of about twenty feet from the rough to the pin. You hit a fine shot and make par. Having overcome any early jitters, you are very excited to get to the next hole and are anxious to start talking about business. You want a sale. Should you be the one to start talking about business?

    A. Why not? Both of you know that this golf round is really about business anyway.

    B. Let the guest bring up the subject.

    C. Wait until after another hole or two, then bring up business.

Score (Par 4)
5: A is a bogey. The reason you're playing is known to both of you, so just let it be. Realize that the guest, though it may not be said now or even later, is appreciative of being

7

asked to play with you. Do not lose sight of this. If there were no interest whatsoever, the client or prospect would not have taken you up on the invitation. Golf takes a lot of time. Don't rush the sale. Let the guest bring up the subject.

3: B is the birdie. Why rush the obvious? Why press it? You want the invited guest to be the one to draw attention to the business matter you wish to discuss. It may not come up on the first hole, the eighth hole or the eighteenth hole. So what? You still have the post-round socializing — the nineteenth hole. Even once you've been seated and the meal has been served, the best time to bring up business may be after the golf round has been discussed. But do not expect it. If anything, just make an appointment for a meeting.

4: C is a par. It is best to let the guest bring up the subject of business first. Why not you? Think about it. If you were the guest, how would you feel? It is only the first hole, so lighten up and give your sales pitch a rest. Have patience and drop out of your sales mode. Encourage the guest to do the talking. Make it a relaxed atmosphere that will create an openness for discussion. The guest is there to enjoy a round of golf and already realizes business is a reason why he or she is there.

Focusing on the Big Picture

In 1980, the American political landscape was changing with a new President. Jack Nicklaus, at age 40, roared back to golf prominence with his masterful victories in the United States Open and the Professional Golf Association championship.

In the very same year, in upstate New York, I had just become a partner in a manufacturing business after eight years in the financial services industry (most of the time in the insurance and banking fields). The company made products for the telecommunications industry.

The business had its origins back in New York City, the result of three people who had a dream to start their own business. Their idea was to blend their work experience as machinists. They needed to purchase machinery and equipment to make products for their commercial clients. Financially, the capital was not available so they talked to some friends and obtained the needed support. But the business failed within a year due to lack of profitable sales.

Despite this setback, none of them could shake off the idea of jointly owning a company. So they saved whatever money they could, learned from their mistakes and remained determined to open another business. They did so a short time later.

The business was very demanding. A couple of years went by, business increased, and they were finally able to quit their daytime jobs to take dead aim at their own business enterprise.

Despite the many ups and downs, sales grew, as did overhead. The years rolled on and the hiring of qualified, responsible and dedicated employees became a key ingredient to their success. The dream of having their own successful business had finally come true. But something was missing.

During a meeting with their accountant, it was suggested that they take up an activity such as golf. The idea was to take some breaks, get away from it all, meet other people and maybe, just maybe, do a little business on the golf links.

Business and golf. Interesting, but would it work? One of the partners heeded the advice, took golf lessons and began playing for the first time. Golf though, like business, was definitely a challenge.

But it worked. By joining an area golf club and playing with others, good and bad experiences came quickly. It took time to develop the golf game and understand it. It was similar to starting a business.

Tips

Many businesses have a dream or mission statement that illustrates the purpose of their existence and their goals. Does your business effectively communicate its goals and purpose? The following tips are suggested for either creating or reviewing your business purpose.

- *Company mission statement:* It is not necessary to invest many thousands of dollars to create one or hire a consulting firm to put one together for you. Do it yourself. Make it an achievable working overall strategy. For example, "The GLF company's purpose is to produce hardware, increase market share in the hardware industry, and grow by offering the highest quality product in the marketplace."

- *Keep it simple and in perspective:* Those in top management and leadership positions set the tone and direction of a company. It is critical that there is a clear vision, real and challenging goals that are specific and understandable. Jack Welch, the chairman and chief executive of General Electric, is a master of this concept. Despite the large size of his company, he has achieved outstanding performances from his employees by using clear and simple messages. A lot of words tend to lead to a lot of clutter and confusion. Remove them! The benefits are in faster and effective decision making.

■ *Boosting workers' self-confidence:* Once the mission and goals are clearly understood, encourage workers' self-confidence by keeping the top management and leadership structure clear, focused and simplified. Establish a creative work environment. Have measurable goals that are realistic, achievable and that have a time line associated with it. Encourage employees to explore ways to do things better on their own within the goals of the company.

■ *Focus on the big picture:* It is common to become too close to the daily operations of the business. Take a step back. Review your plans. Talk with the employees. Target your key customers and why they do business with your company. Delegate work and figure out how your company can maximize its strengths.

Summary

One way to free up time for an activity such as business-to-business golf is by reviewing your overall goals and purpose. Who would you target among your existing and potential customer base for increased business? How important is this to your business? Will it result in new contacts, relationships and opportunities? How much time are you willing to take to become proficient in business-to-business golf?

FULLY EQUIPPED
How to Know What's Good For You

2nd HOLE: A couple of weeks ago, you purchased a set of golf clubs. One reason you made the investment was for this second hole. You have played the hole often. It is a short par four and has a lot of rough. Before playing today, you spent considerable time practicing at the driving range with your new equipment. Despite this effort, your tee shot landed deep into heavy rough about forty yards out from the green. You are annoyed that you did not practice this type of shot earlier, and you are even partially blaming the clubs. Should you:

A. Decide to take a lot of extra practice swings since this shot creates a lot of pressure on you.

B. Take a lot of time to size up the shot even if it means slowing up play a little. Your guest won't mind since this is a free round. Plus, you are still not used to the new clubs.

C. Don't take much time. Take one practice swing, if you need to, and no more. Do not keep your guest or any golfer waiting.

Score (Par 4)

4: A is par but keep it limited to no more than one practice swing for time consideration and speed of play! Consider the following about practicing before a business-to-business golf round: practice minimally, just enough to warm up, by taking a dozen or less practice shots at the practice range. Too many business-to-business golf players feel it is necessary to hit a lot of extra practice shots before play. The result is a long workout, the buildup of a lot of sweat, and possibly becoming frustrated. Why? Is it to get into a proper rhythm, overcome self-doubts, or hit the great final shot before playing? Forget it! Save energy, sweat and mental fatigue! If you think you will all of a sudden find a secret to golf success or the ideal swing, chances are you will not. The time to practice intensely is not just prior to a business-to-business golf outing. It is too late. Don't do it! Instead, accept the swing you have and what you already know. Relax. Hit only a handful of shots and practice a few chips and putts. No more! If you do a lot more, you may wipe yourself out (mentally and physically) before the first tee shot! Practice has its own separate time place and that is definitely not when playing business-to-business golf.

5: B is a bogey since it assumes your guest will not mind. This could be a major error in judgment. Time is a precious commodity, particularly when playing golf. It is not fun to wait especially if you are the one at fault. Short delays add up quickly. Your guest, in all likelihood, will notice and will not care what you paid for today. The guest owes you nothing. A key ingredient to making favorable impressions is to take minimal time for each golf shot. The guest will appreciate it very much, as will the other players in your group, and those who are playing in the group behind you.

And, don't blame the new clubs, since it may just be an adjustment period you are going through!

3: C is a birdie and shows you have purpose. This truly earns you respect. No words can take the place of your actions.

How to Know What's Good for You

Whether you work in the service or manufacturing industry, having the appropriate equipment is essential. For example, in my manufacturing business, our firm's telecommunications products for test equipment had a unique requirement. Our commercial and government customers mandated a feature in each of our units, a built-in, back-up warning signal. Since test equipment was used in a variety of environments it was important to make sure that it functioned under virtually any circumstance, especially when our product was part of an overall communication network.

In manufacturing the item, it was very important for production operations to maintain tight quality control. This assured product integrity and that customer specifications were met. It was imperative for us to invest in quality equipment. We regularly experimented to see if we could improve our production capacity. We visited other companies, researched, and even tried to emulate the operations of other companies with similar products. But in the end, we could only do what was best for our situation by purchasing the best equipment for our needs. We stressed quality and performance in order to produce a good and reliable product time and time again.

In the service industry, needs are great, and computer equipment is high on the list. But to automate for automation's sake may not be good. Costs may increase, not so much for the equipment, but for the personnel time involved. In purchasing a computer information system, for example, there are many variables. Make a list of what you wish to obtain from your system. Can you use existing software and hardware to leverage the situation? What kind of support, training, and expertise is required? Can you properly manage it? What kind of reporting will be generated? Which departments and personnel are to receive them and what happens with the information being supplied?

It is possible to have too much information that is not relevant to the task at hand. The key is to make sure that the appropriate technology for your situation will be able to provide solutions. Who receives the information? Is it going to better service customers, enable you to enter new markets, keep a competitive edge and make your company more efficient and productive? Will the information technology system make it easier for employees to do their work, or just create more unnecessary paperwork that will never be used?

Tips

Many companies review their business practices and processes with the goal of investing in appropriate technology and equipment. From computers to machinery, it is critical that your company has the necessary personnel and support to harness the productivity gains that are expected. How will the information be reported internally and how does it benefit the customer? Have you done the following within the past six to twelve months?

■ Maintain and periodically update a facilities checklist. List all equipment, whether owned or leased, with date of purchase, history of service or repairs, warranty information, receipts, vendor information and reason for purchase.

■ Make each department head responsible for the information collected. Make it subject to review by top management. Encourage equipment upgrades, ask for comments and have cost figures available for any purchase decision. Each piece of equipment should have its maintenance schedule, manufacturer, telephone number, website address, and who to call in case of an emergency located both on the equipment and in a database.

■ If you are a manufacturer, list the products or parts produced per hour and labor time involved, along with the percentage of parts rejected. If in the service industry, list the time impact on labor. Also, ask yourself if the equipment location is fairly accessible or if it can be improved.

■ What software program reports are key for each department and to whom do they go? What information is essential to each area? Is there redundancy or time wasted reviewing non-essential information?

■ For computer information systems, what equipment, peripherals or devices are needed? Why not go to www.zdnet.net or www.tucows.com as a starting point to help with the selection process?

Summary

How much time can you save by obtaining the proper and productive equipment? What is the payback period? Will it help generate more time for finding or developing business relationships, especially on the golf course?

A PLACE TO BE
Location... Location... Location

3ʳᵈ HOLE: The golf course you are playing is a draw for many players due to its proximity to a sizable golfing population and a reputation for good appearance, care and condition. You are taken by surprise when your guest takes a sizable divot after hitting an iron from the fairway and purposely leaves it without making an attempt to replace it. Should you:

A. Make an effort to say something about replacing it.

B. Just let it be and do nothing since you may embarrass the guest.

C. Replace the divot immediately for the guest.

Score (Par 3)

3: A is a par if you do mention that the divot needs to be replaced. Take care of the course whether it is your home course or any other place. It is a cardinal rule in golf to replace your own divots. Grass that is removed by a golf shot and not replaced takes a long time to grow back. A lot of care and investment goes into maintaining the course—just ask any golf course superintendent. Consider the effort involved and set the example. Repair and replace each divot. Develop the habit of fixing an indentation made on the putting green surface by a golf shot. After all, you may prevent yourself from becoming the victim of a damaged area. Take pride in the golf course you are playing and voluntarily replace or fix up the turf as needed. Your actions speak in a high volume. Your guest will take notice.

4: B scores a bogey since no action is taken by anyone to repair the course. This is bad news and shows a lack of care, concern and character. You will not embarrass anyone by taking the appropriate action. It will only enhance your stature.

2: C shows responsibility, which is definitely a good thing. Words do not have to be spoken. Just doing it sends the message—you score a birdie.

Location...Location...Location

Many real estate people insist that location is the key for future value. The financial service companies I worked for each had good office facilities for conducting customer interviews and meetings. If you were to visit the original site of my manufacturing business in the early eighties, you would probably notice that the structure dated back to the 1920s. It was presentable. For our line of work, the business did not require a prime location; we simply needed space. But we were cramped and it affected our productivity. Our equipment, inventory, assembly area and offices were very congested. We rented space on two floors, and no matter what we did to reorganize or rearrange, the limited space resulted in a lot of inefficiencies.

For example, inventory was all over the place and spread into too many diverse areas, including the entrance lobby and rest rooms. Parts for subassemblies, all too often, could not be found. We worked overtime to be sure we had the parts needed, conducted inventory, sorted out the good parts from bad, and made sure we could meet delivery against orders. But the root cause of the problem had to be addressed.

Despite the costs involved, we nevertheless started the search for a new place of business. After several visits to a number of companies and reviewing several layout plans for a new facility, we found property that would be a good site. It was not far from our operations and would be a sound investment for the future. It would enable us to grow our business.

The financial industry traditionally selects fairly visible locations for the convenience of clients and to attract new customers. The growth of the Internet and the encouragement to shop and conduct transactions from one's own computer may change the physical demands of having to have a premium location in the future.

Creating the right physical corporate environment is important to many employees, particularly when recruiting new ones. Keep the location as presentable as possible. Doing a little landscaping certainly helps but it does not need to be a major expense. It may help recruit good people and indicate to them that you take a certain amount of care and pride at your place of business.

Tips

How presentable is your place of work? When was the last time you conducted a review of the building, property, maintenance and upkeep? Are you proud of it? Do you have enough room? Can you reorganize and create more space? Will a better layout increase efficiency? Consider the following:

■ How is your office or plant organized for materials and flow of work? Should certain equipment be relocated? Is there excessive inventory taking up too much space? Do you have a layout plan that you can review or have one created? How safe is your place of business?

■ Draw an outline—take some photographs from a good distance away and develop a flow of work diagram or processing charts. This will help you view your surroundings from a different perspective and see how things might be changed.

■ Before purchasing or leasing any new equipment, picture how it would work in your environment. Ask the vendor if there is a place you can see the equipment or at least visualize it at your facility. Consider others costs such as installation, added features, etc.

■ Service industries need to review the efficiency of their operation especially from the customer's point of view. Though the Internet is encouraging clients to conduct more business online to help companies reduce costs, the physical presence of the customer is still a key factor. How often do you have prospects or clients visit your office? Is it a deterrent to sales? Are you more productive by having clients or prospects visit your place of business?

Summary

Do you feel good about the location of your place of business? Does it provide you with a good environment, especially for visitors? How much is it worth to you to have a clean place? Public or private golf courses are generally in good or excellent condition. Take a look around and see if you can borrow some appearance ideas from the golf course for your place of business.

SIZING UP THE SITUATION
Knowing Your Strengths...
and Weaknesses

4th HOLE: In order to size up a situation on the putting green, you want to see the direction of a putt being taken by your guest, who is hitting first. You have been in the habit of standing behind your guest on the putting green for most of the putts. However, you realize by your guest's body movement that you may have been standing a little too close in this instance. Your guest is lining up the putt and about to stroke the ball. What is the best thing to do?

A. Since nothing has been said, keep standing behind your guest.

B. Immediately back away and apologize.

C. There is no reason to change, but it is probably a good idea to back away a safe distance starting at the next hole.

Score (Par 5)

6: A is not good. What a good way to annoy a golfer, let alone a client or prospect for your business! This is a bogey and well deserved—it should be a even higher score. This is near the top of the aggravation list.

25

4: B is a birdie since it shows that you recognize your mistake. This shows that you are responsible. It takes away any possibility that the guest will see you as purposely trying to take advantage of the situation. Any advantage is not worth the problem it may pose to you later, especially if your guest says something. Besides, it is against golf rules.

5: C is a par. You bet it is a good idea to back away. Go even a little further back than might be necessary, just to be safe. This shows you are sensitive to your guest's needs and willing to adapt and make the change. It is a rule of golf that you are not allowed to stand directly behind the player.

Knowing Your Strengths ... and Weaknesses

My company moved into a larger facility providing us with needed space, expansion capability and greater efficiency. However, we still needed help to plan things out, assess certain situations, and review our unique weaknesses and strengths. Many times, there was a feeling of being too close to a situation and unable to see an obvious problem. This hit home for me since I had a direct financial stake in the outcome of our operations each year. It was not so direct with the insurance since it was primarily commission based and I had no financial ownership.

Today, in most states throughout the United States, there is a Manufacturing Extension Program (MEP) Center that is designed to serve virtually every business. These organizations are affiliated with the Department of Commerce's National Institute of Standards & Technology. MEP Centers work with businesses to help them reduce costs, run more profitably and become more competitive. The MEP Centers are independent and can help a business assess itself and implement changes necessary for improvement. They maintain a nationwide resource database. Fees are reasonable. In fact, not all Centers charge fees for each service provided. They may also use private consultants. To contact a Center, call 1-800-MEP4MFG (1-800-637-4634).

In our case, we needed to review our plant layout and productivity, and find new markets. An assessment was made of our major business functions. Key people of each department were interviewed and a review as the information obtained helped to assess the overall effectiveness of the business. Recommendations were made for the implementation of necessary changes. You may be able to make some changes yourself, have the MEP do it for you, or implement change through a third-party provider or private consultant. The program has helped many businesses focus on being more productive, competitive and profitable.

In financial services, it is important to join industry groups or associations, take continuing education courses and regularly take note of any changes to products being offered for your clients so your customers can obtain the type of plan best for their situation. As an example, many times I conducted a needs analysis to determine the amount of life and disability insurance, if any, that would be needed by a client. The analysis was an objective financial look at assets, liabilities and government programs that would apply. It often created a healthy conversation, provided good information and invariably showed the strong and weak points in one's financial plan.

Knowing your own strengths and weaknesses, regardless of the industry you are involved in, keeps you updated and creates awareness of the issues. The key is to follow through on any plan or get the needed help to implement change. Be sure to focus on the main issues and ask what reasons exist to support certain conclusions. Are vague statements being made? If so, question them. Are there issues that are especially worrisome or keeping you up at night? Are they sales, financial, expenses, hiring people, competition? What is your top priority?

Qualified independent third-party providers or consultants bring objectivity and can help assess or analyze your company or individual situation. Do not expect consultants, however, to be magicians and bring in a instant formula to successfully increase profitable sales by a high percentage, particularly if your industry has little growth expectation. But do have the work scope and report put in writing as much as possible, covering the issue(s) you are working with, the action necessary to resolve them and how you want to receive it (formal report, software presentation or in a meeting).

Tips

In any assessment, particularly for a manufacturing concern, the following areas should be included as appropriate: management, human resource, sales, marketing, production, financial, operations, and quality. Some of the strengths and weaknesses cited in the audit may be a tip-off for you to take a fresh look at your situation.

Have an outside third party or consultant interview not only yourself, but also your key employees. Many times there are other underlying issues that may truly be the cause of the problem. Since the consultant is not part of your company, he or she can provide an unbiased and objective picture.

Qualified consultants are an excellent source of information. They may tell you things that you may not want to hear. That's good. Be wary of those who may tell you only what the company wants to hear. In addition to identifying issues, or confirming things you may already know, they can often implement the solution or suggest the appropriate qualified resource.

Keep a schedule and know your costs up front with a consultant. Be sure details are covered by asking questions and thinking through each side of a problem. You may even wish to benchmark or compare your company to industry standards such as financials. Robert Morris is a recognized name in financial benchmarking, for example, and can be reached at www.rmahq.com. Review the confidentiality of your information and the use of it.

Summary

Can a review of strengths and weakness generate a new focus for your business? Who would you consider to assist you in this process? Are there professionals who may be members of an area organization, golf club or association that can be of help?

Even in playing golf, are there caddies where you play? Do you ever hire one? Rather than riding a golf car, use a caddy whenever possible. He or she can provide you with valuable observations and advice.

How about for your own golf game? Are you experiencing difficulties or would you just like to fine tune it? See your local golf professional and talk it out with a lesson. The professional has spent many years learning his or her skill and has a vested interest in helping you. He or she can also provide an expert opinion for which clubs and equipment are best for your swing and game. Many professionals are members of other organizations and associations and may be eligible to play in and invite you to other events, functions and tournaments. These can be very valuable networking opportunities. Treat the professional as your partner in your golf game, business-to-business golf outings and meeting new people.

5

PEOPLE AND PRODUCTIVITY
Living Up to Your Skills

5th HOLE: While waiting to tee off, your guest mentions how difficult it is to find good employees. You agree and suggest a couple of firms that deal with hiring people and agree to follow up with a couple of referrals. You are pleased that you are in a position to help. In fact, you are so excited you switch the conversation to the last hole where your guest had hit a bad golf shot. You try to help by pointing out what the problem was and giving a mini-lesson even though you were not asked to do so.

    A. Don't give out any advice unless asked.

    B. Say something positive and suggest the next hole will be better.

    C. You feel your guest needs help and you decide to provide advice.

Score (Par 4)
3: A is a birdie. Let the guest come to you for help! I repeat, let the guest ask you first. If you are not sure what to say, say so. If you have a good idea or feel you can help, go for it.

31

Do not worry if the advice works. Whether it does or not is immaterial. State your case once and let it be. You will know either during the round or afterwards if it produced results, but try to emphasize that it is best to practice any suggestions rather than experimenting while playing. This is, in effect, a disclaimer that will keep you protected from any negative fallout from the shot with which you were asked to help.

4: B is closer but try not to offer suggestions. A positive word is okay, but keep it short and to the point without having to explain anything. You score a par.

5: C scores a bogey. As much as you may want to help, do not volunteer any advice unless asked. Why not? First of all, the guest may not want your advice! Secondly, despite good intentions, you may make he or she feel inferior to you and that is no good. Lastly, the guest may try what you said and chances are the shot may not work out at all since there is no opportunity to practice it first. The rule is not to give out advice unless you are specifically asked. Otherwise, it may work against you.

Living Up to Your Skills

Each company I worked for had a substantial investment in building, property, office equipment and computers. My own business had a large investment in the property and building, plus tooling, machinery, inventory and information system. But the most important assets were the people. The intangibles that are a part of the human condition — attitude, work ethic, drive, encouragement and enthusiasm are the driving forces for just about every company. The leadership, from top management throughout the various departments, develop the atmosphere and culture of the business. A good flow of communication certainly helps.

Many times, especially when I worked in financial services, personnel problems developed due to personality clashes, disagreements and misunderstandings. In my own business, we encouraged training and allowed flexibility with work hours as needed in an effort to help with productivity. There were times when productivity spiked due to sudden orders, emergencies, crises and meeting deadlines at the last possible hour. This is not the best way to make things happen, though it did provide for interesting times.

We had annual increases with provisions for merit raises, holiday breaks and occasional social get-togethers. This helped morale. But do you know what employees want most from work? Is it job security? Good wages? Appreciation for the work they do? Promotions? Loyalty? An article in the *Investor's Business Daily,* said that the number one priority as to what employees want most from their job—according to company managers—was good wages. What does the *employee* say? Is it good wages, too? No. The top priority is being fully appreciated for their work.

The message is quite clear. Pay attention to your workers and what they are doing. Learn from them as they do from you. Encourage conversation. More often than not, they will help you with good advice or ideas, recruiting new employees and identifying the type of workers you need. People want to feel that they are contributing, involved and thought of by others, especially their superiors and top management.

Do you know what it costs to replace or hire a worker? Studies indicate that it is much more than just salary, benefits and time for interviewing. There are other factors, such as ads placed in newspapers, trade magazines, or associations; payment for using a recruiter; the loss or gain of business by the individual who is being replaced; lost sales; customer complaints; productivity; and miscellaneous (non-business time on the computer, excessive conversation, and meetings, etc.). Costs for replacing key personnel vary, but can be as much as one's yearly salary. Maybe more. Maybe less. What does it cost your company for the position or positions being considered?

Review the position first and see if anything has changed. Obtain as much information as possible from others and the person who may be vacating the job, if appropriate. When interviewing a candidate, have the applicable department head be a part of the interviewing process from the very beginning. If seriously considering hiring the applicant, verify references, and schedule another interview. Review the candidate's resume and see if the information flows with the dates, checking for time or employment gaps. Be sure the resume is presented in a clear and understandable sequence of events.

The interview process requires key questions not only about job skills and knowledge but also how an employee may respond in given situations. Encourage the candidate to talk as much as possible about their skills and experience. This helps to see how he or she would fit into the environment. Ask for details and specific examples. Pay attention to their reactions, especially tone of voice, body language, eye contact (or lack of) and facial expressions.

This could help you to pursue further questioning and keep control of the interview.

Upon completion of the interview, write down your impressions immediately. This is the best time because you will remember the most information. Write as many notes as possible, including whether or not this candidate would be suitable for hiring. If there was another interviewer, include her or his comments and opinions.

Once hired, have the new employee learn about company history and what you do. With low unemployment and the current difficulty of finding capable and productive people, it is essential to have an employee learn as much as they can about their job description, responsibilities, communication channels and what the expectations are. Show that your business encourages input, creativity, ideas and suggestions. It adds to a good working environment which helps increase one's productivity. Employees will have a high interest level and may be more loyal when given attention, and consideration. Making them feel appreciated will cause them to feel good about themselves and your company.

Tips

Do you cross-train employees and help them learn other aspects of the company that would fit in with their skills? Do you know the full capabilities of your employees? When was the last time you reviewed their job descriptions? Consider the following:

■ For people who have been working for a period of time, how do you rate their job performance? Does the employee have a job description, and if so, does it fit? Has the job changed substantially? Where does employee excel or where does he or she fall short? Have examples to stress key points you wish to make during a job performance review. You may wish to visit www.keepem.com regarding retaining good workers.

■ When was the last time you reviewed each employee's job skills versus their job description? Does their job description match their daily work? Is it time for a refresher course, new training, or a move into a different role?

■ When observing your work force, note their attitude —is it positive or negative? How do they feel about themselves? Are they willing to learn? How energetic or enthusiastic are they? Do they have a drive to succeed in their work? How is their attitude? Productivity can be affected in a major way here since it is, after all, represented by the amount of work output for each hour on the job.

The above observations also apply when interviewing candidates for employment. Ask plenty of questions to keep the interviewee talking. Do you get a sense that they have good self-esteem? What has been their greatest challenge? Do they have a will to succeed? Ask yourself how necessary it is for candidate to have a certain amount of years of experience, or a college degree, to perform the job. Pay attention to the interviewee's personality, ability to communicate and how he or she would fit into your company's environment. Keep a list of things you wish to cover during the interview if necessary.

Summary

Do you skimp on skills training or do you consider it an investment? How much time can you realistically devote for entertaining clients and customers? Do you have an appropriate person or staff who can properly do the job in your place, particularly for business-to-business golf? Do you need to train or role play with others? Is the person qualified, not just as a golfer, but with enough people skills for your comfort?

6

FINDING
OPPORTUNITIES
Communication is the Key

6th HOLE: You are enjoying the day. Your game has been fair but void of any birdie opportunities until this hole. You're on the green putting for a birdie from about twenty-five feet away. Your guest is standing quite close to you and does not seem to realize how much it is bothering your concentration. You wish to communicate using one of the following:

A. Wave your arm at your guest to have him or her move a little and say nothing.

B. In a pleasant way, ask your guest to move away since it is bothering you.

C. Don't rock the boat since this is an important client and you do not want to miss any sale opportunities. Go ahead and putt.

Score (Par 4)

4: A is a par. You should say something in a positive manner, not crudely, and state your appreciation for moving away from your line of putt. If it is still not enough, say it again. Do not be bashful or feel that you cannot do so. It is a smart move and indicates you are not afraid to make such a request. This is a character builder for both you and the guest.

3: B shows diplomacy and not being afraid or hesitant to point out something that is amiss. This is a birdie for you.

5: C indicates a possible weakness that the customer may notice and rates a bogey. Most likely, the client knows what he or she is doing. It could be a test to see how you would react. If you say nothing and putt when it first happens, it will repeat itself again and again. It could haunt you for the rest of the business-to-business golf round.

Communication Is the Key

Unlike the insurance business, which is known for its sales representatives, or banking with its relationship managers, our manufacturing business did not employ any formal salespeople. We had our inside customer service personnel, contract administrators, troubleshooters and technicians, but no direct sales people or even sales representatives.

How did we generate sales? As a principal of the firm, I made it my work to contact customers and prospects to obtain repeat business and leads. Attending trade shows, seminars and conferences provided good networking opportunities for sales and support. This was very similar to insurance and banking where involvement with business groups such as the Chamber of Commerce, community boards of directors, not-for-profit organizations, and others play an important role in making one's presence known.

For years, our company's sales growth was triggered, in part, by our reputation for quality and prompt delivery. "Make the product right the first time" was our battle cry. We emphasized sales support when problems arose. We took corrective action with the customer. Rapid response generated good public relations and resolved complaints.

Additionally, the company believed it was very important to do periodic customer surveys to see how we were doing. We wanted to determine from the customer's point of view if what we thought was accurate. We believed our way of doing business would automatically lead to sales. We felt we could beat our competition. But there was always a doubt. Through our survey, we would uncover some interesting news, leads, or even an order. If there was trouble and we were losing out, we needed to know. Some businesses could not understand why they lost a bid. They would not even ask!

Bids, sales and surveys were combined into one customer survey conducted on a regular basis mostly by telephone. It was also important to ask about our quality and delivery as well as industry trends. In effect, we were using our customers as advisors.

When reviewing survey results, we braced ourselves for some hard truths; yet, these surveys became an opportunity for sales. Though we conducted a lot of the surveys, companies should caution themselves against administering a customer survey on their own. I often felt the customer did not respond honestly for fear of offending us or possibly feeling some pressure not to say anything. This was not true all of the time, of course; some clients will take advantage of the situation to complain about product price. It was also important not to take any negative comments personally. It may be more productive to have an outside, objective third party conduct a customer satisfaction survey. This tends to take away bias and provide the customer the opportunity to disclose more information.

We made it a point to maintain good communication with buyers of commodity items and to spot any trends or relevant

41

news that might impact us. We retained an outside consultant to regularly monitor related items which helped provide new bidding opportunities on related products and an understanding of the marketplace.

Tips

When was the last time your company conducted a customer satisfaction survey? Did it uncover any new business opportunities? What kind of format did you use? Who did it and what questions were asked? Consider the following areas:

Customer surveys should address your company's primary concerns. Quality of product or service, delivery and responsiveness are key areas. Remember, dissatisfied customers tell more people about their experience with your company than satisfied customers do. Uncover those dissatisfied ones as quickly as possible and visit them. There may be other reasons for dissatisfaction, and questions of honesty and integrity may be a part of it. Be prepared.

Among the items we discovered in the survey was that our customers normally expected responses to their inquiries within forty-eight hours. What are your customers' expectations for responsiveness? Do you respond to your customer quickly even if you may not have a direct answer? Do you indicate to your customer how long it will take to get a response?

The decision to conduct customer surveys should come from top management and requires the entire company's commitment. The customer satisfaction survey should start with an advance notice, preferably by one-page fax, to let the customer know he or she will be contacted by telephone in one week. The actual call should focus on no more than five key areas. Keep the time of each call to approximately ten to fifteen minutes; and state this at the beginning of the call. Encourage the customer to talk and ask any follow-up questions as needed. It is best to call at non-peak times, such as early in the morning, lunch time or at the end of the day. If your customer is busy, ask for the best time to call back. Be sure to emphasize the confidentiality of the conversation and create a relaxed and amicable atmosphere.

Have questions prepared and organized. Time goes by quickly during the interview and the flow of information may not follow the script you have. Check off the areas that have been discussed so you can go back as needed. Take detailed notes and ask to repeat when necessary. Do not rush. Ask probing questions, but be aware of the time elapsed.

In the service industry, how do you find sales opportunities? By servicing clients? Do you know your particular strengths and weaknesses against your competition? Why clients buy from you in the first place? Do you regularly service your customers and truly attempt to understand their needs? If you see an article in a newspaper, magazine or on the Internet that might be of interest, do you send it? Has your company conducted customer surveys that you can review?

Does your company coordinate efforts among the sales team, business development group, sales manager and top management? Is there discussion regarding the issues that are most important to your clients? Is there any role playing —to simulate the customer and anticipate their concerns? Learn to understand your clientele or prospects and to put yourself in their position. How often do you ask for referrals? Thank those who help you.

Participate in golf outings, particularly those with charitable causes, and even become involved in planning these events as much as possible. Consider having your company sponsor an event or having an outing. It does not have to be large amount of people. Invite several foursomes (about four to six foursomes will work). It is similar to conducting a seminar, where the smaller sizes (up to fifteen to twenty people) provide greater one-on-one communication, and a larger size may be too much.

If you host your own golf event or become a sponsor, ask yourself what your expectations are or what you hope to accomplish. Are you offering anything new, such as a new product or service? Or is the purpose to thank customers or reward productive employees? Establish a budget and select a committee to help you. Utilize the services of the golf professional at the club where the event is being held and incorporate his or her ideas about the prizes and planning of the day. Support the club professional by purchasing golf prizes and gift certificates. You will have professional results. Also, meet with the club's general manager for scheduling and overall coordination. It is not unusual to obtain approval from a Board or Committee for your event. The key for a successful outing is organization and delegation of responsibilities. It may take as little as a few weeks or as much as many months to organize a good event, depending on the size of the field. Planning for an event includes items such as the food selection, sponsor signs to be placed out on the course, arrangement for any celebrities, access to clubhouse, golf lessons or exhibitions, handicap format, registration, giveaways, raffles and other items. Work it from a team approach, and make sure the responsibilities and costs are established as early as possible.

Also, if you are inviting an associate from your company or from another firm to play with you and your business-to-business golf guest, you may want to do your own kind of survey. Take time to review to see who would be an appropriate fit. There are many types of business-to-business golfers. An attempt has been made to list three types. Whoever you ask to play, review the reason why the business-to-business golf round is being scheduled and who has been invited. If there is a reason to involve this person to help you make any of the arrangements for the golf date, review what needs to be done and set a time for a follow-up. People are different and have their own style, personality and ways of doing things. Carefully review the listing below. It is not suggesting that you or anyone else become one type of business-to-business golfer or another. Simply review it and visualize whether your associate or other firm would or would not be a good fit to play business-to-business golf with your guest:

■ *Freewheeling:* An "anything-goes" type of business-to-business golfer. He or she lacks full knowledge and appreciation of the etiquette and rules to properly conduct business-to-business golf. This is not necessarily a negative as long as the intent and desire is there to improve. Tends to be late and disorganized. Practices only as needed and then it is intense. Plays business-to-business golf with anyone and recognizes the value of building a relationship, but needs a lot of follow-up help in preparation for a meaningful business-to-business golf round.

■ *Functional:* This type of business-to-business golfer goes strictly by the book, is quite rigid and views business-to-business golf more as an obligation. He or she will do what they have to do and not exercise much creativity, let alone show any emotion or enjoyment, and not make a major effort to establish a good rapport with the guest. Not easily impressed by the customer's position. Will arrive on time and leave as scheduled. He or she will practice only minimally. Needs no help to plan out the business-to-business golf day.

■ *Focused:* This business-to-business golfer is very serious about the game and competitive. There is a preference to play with guests who have a similar golf handicap or better and desire to align themselves with those who have prestigious company positions. Arrives early and practices his or her golf game a lot before the round starts, but is insensitive to guest needs. Focused more on self than on the guest. They need some assistance in scheduling and planning for business-to-business golf.

Summary

How many sales opportunities have you capitalized on? Or missed? Can you quantify this? Have lessons been learned? Have you fully serviced your client? Have you shown your appreciation for her or his business? Would you have your own special golf day or event? Who would be the most appropriate person to help plan it or be a part of your golfing group?

EXPECTING THE UNEXPECTED
No More Surprises

7th HOLE: Your guest tees up and strikes the ball with a four iron. The ball goes relatively high. Nothing special but it looks like a good shot. It is heading toward the pin. The ball lands on the front part of the green, takes one bounce, and goes into the cup! A hole-in-one! An ace! An eagle! A score of one! Unbelievable. Incredible. The guest is ecstatic and runs to the green in excitement to take the ball out of the hole. Too bad this was not a tournament to get a good prize. However, it is customary for the one who makes a hole-in-one to buy the drinks. Should you:

    A. Let the guest buy the drinks for everyone.

    B. Insist on paying for the bill since it is your club and you would be honored to do so.

    C. Forget about it once the celebration dies down since there are a number of holes you still have to play.

Score (Par 3)
3: A is a par and the ordinary thing to do. But why have your guest pay at your club? If he or she insists that may be one thing, but make the offer anyway.

2: B is a birdie since you are pleased not only to witness such a shot but able to share in the celebration. The gesture of picking up the bill shows your excitement for the guest and may be a moot point anyway. A lot of clubs may not allow cash—just charges. So take the first step even if there are not that many people around. It will not matter much anyway. In fact, after the round is completed, send him or her a certificate of recognition on your company letterhead. Ask the pro shop if there are anyone other prizes for which your guest may be eligible. Note: You may wish to do this for an eagle score on a par four or par five hole.

4: C is a bogey and denial. It shows no special effort for such a special shot. How would you feel if the situation were reversed? Make it even more memorable by talking about it to others with the guest present as appropriate.

No More Surprises

The banking and insurance businesses I worked in enjoyed steady growth. The manufacturing company was different. We experienced a serious upward movement in sales once we completed the move into the larger new facility. We were now able to bring in a new complementary product line. Sales for our core telecommunication products were steady and gave our business a sense of security. But this was not all good. We needed to keep a more watchful eye within our industry, for the unexpected can and does happen.

Our products were highly dependent upon the test and monitoring equipment market. The military was also a good customer, and the upward trend in defense spending, along with our firm's commercial account base, was a definite plus. The growth in the marketplace was a welcome set of circumstances. It was based on our country's desire at the time to strengthen its armed forces. As a result, more sales led to more jobs and many of our commercial customers anticipated even more increases in orders for years to come.

The strategy of strengthening the military forces and the influence of Pope John Paul II helped to facilitate the destruction of the Berlin Wall in Germany and the collapse of the Soviet Union. Peace through strength worked. These were truly surprising developments. Who could have foreseen this just a few short years prior? And something else happened quite unexpectedly—a rippling effect that would reverse the trend of increasing sales for our company. With the great confrontation between the two superpowers now over, the military reduced its levels of spending. Unknown to the industry at the time, we were at the beginning of a period of reduced product demand that would last for a few years. Although business became more competitive, new opportunities would enter the picture as government accounts moved towards purchasing more items that were available right off the shelf, a process known as commercialization.

This became a positive development and helped reduce overhead costs. Sales increased. Yet throughout this entire situation, the key for us was the ability to provide good quality products for a reasonable price with on-time delivery. We were fortunate to receive awards recognizing our products' quality from several of our customers.

After these experiences, it dawned on me that I had to make a plan and prepare for the worst case scenario. The unexpected can occur at any time and it is not enough just to know your industry. Face your fears. Know your strengths and weaknesses. Keep your company prepared for the lean times so you will be better prepared for the unexpected.

Tips

Does your company have provisions set aside for the lean times or unexpected situations that may negatively affect cash flow? Whether you are a manufacturer or in the service sector, here are a few suggestions:

- Set up a separate line item in your budget for a "reserve fund," just as you do for regular monthly payments such as utilities, loan payments, leases, telephone, and so on. Take a percentage of gross sales for the month, for example 1% to 3% or more, and deposit it into this fund. Treat it as a payment to your company for your overall efforts and accumulate enough for emergencies or opportunities.

- Use unexpected savings, discounts from suppliers, vendors or overhead for your reserve fund. Make sure, however, your purchasing department is continuously seeking the most favorable discount terms, purchasing at appropriate cash flow intervals, and verifying inventory accuracy and lead times.

- Review your regular overhead costs for insurance, telephone, software, and copier for billing accuracy. Check your invoices carefully before mailing a payment and know who you are dealing with— stay with reputable suppliers and vendors. If your company has been taken advantage of with improper billings, report the incident to the Federal Trade Commission (FTC) Consumer Response Center at

1-877-FTC-HELP. Review these costs using your own internal personnel or hire a specialist who can assist in each area. Many cost reduction specialists work on a contingency basis; they receive a portion of your savings for a period of time, such as one or two years.

- How are your account receivables? When working with a new client, obtain as much information as possible that will help you in the event there are financial concerns down the road. The goal is not to be caught off guard. Know when they would typically make payments and keep a copy of a customer's check upon payment so you have at least some banking information for reference. Keep a list of those who have not paid beyond thirty days and follow up with a phone call. The call may uncover a simple oversight or more importantly, a legitimate reason for lack of payment. If the uncollected receivable persists, and nothing can be worked out such as a series of payments over time, consider contacting a collection expert and the possible use of an attorney.

- What about your own employees or co-workers? Are their personal obligations affecting their work? If so, does it take up a significant amount of time? How is it affecting their work? A lot of lost productivity? A lot of denial? Employee debt covers the entire income range. How can you help? The credit counseling industry helps many people and some resources are available, such as the Association of Independent Consumer Credit Counseling Agencies at www.aiccca.org. A not-for-profit agency such as www.auriton.org may also provide the help needed.

51

■ Looking for deals? Check the federal government. Many different items are regularly sold that may provide you with the best possible deals. From the Defense Department (www.drms.com) to General Services Administration (www.gsa.gov/regions.html) to Treasury Department (treas.gov/auctions/customs) to Federal Deposit Insurance Corp. (www.fdic.gov) to name a few.

Summary

Keep options open. You never know when an opportunity may arise for a game of golf with clients, or with other people who may be good sources of information or a networking opportunity for your business.

ENOUGH IS ENOUGH
You Should Never Assume

8ᵗʰ HOLE: You have had two good holes in a row and have a good score so far. Your second shot finds you just off the fairway in the rough. While addressing the ball, you inadvertently touch the ball with your club and the ball moves from its original position about an inch or so. You know full well that the golf rules mandate a one stroke penalty.

A. Do not worry about it since your guest was on the opposite side of the fairway and could not have possibly noticed.

B. Your intention is to say something but wait until later in the round.

C. You immediately add the penalty to your score and hit the ball. You advise your guest right away of your score.

Score (Par 4)

5: A is a bogey and more. Lying should bother you, if not now, then later. It can also develop into a very bad habit. Though you may be able to cover up, it can disturb any momentum you may have been building with your game and become a distraction to business-to-business golf. Even worse, it may have been noticed by your guest! Why risk it? Look at it this way—it is just one shot added to your score. Take the penalty. Honesty displays character. Being honest gives a greater peace of mind and helps you play a better round since you did the right thing.

4: B is a par. Intentions are good but be sure to state what happened as soon as possible. Do not delay. The guest may wonder why you waited so long, especially if it occurred several holes before. Get it over with and play on!

3: C is a birdie and the best way to go. Hard to believe anyone would do this? Happens more than you may think. By voluntarily assessing yourself an extra stroke, you are not only playing by the rules, you will play with a clear mind and make you feel good. This is also be a plus for your golf since having a good attitude is very important. The guest also will not forget what you did.

You Should Never Assume

I can't tell you how many mistakes and errors in judgment I have made in business, regardless of the industry. It is one thing to be working for an employer and make errors, and quite another to own a business and see mistakes being made. But no matter who is at fault, mistakes need to be dealt with so that they are not repeated.

The work environment depends upon on how top management leads and their willingness to deal with issues in a constructive manner. If management sets a good example and encourages teamwork, communication and openness, employees will respond. No one wants to be embarrassed or humiliated. But things do happen, particularly as situations unfold during a business day. It is important for every employee to know and understand his or her job, and role, how it relates to the company's goals and mission. It is equally important for every employee to have the confidence to address situations without fear and to be fully encouraged to tell the truth. Lies may be the root cause of the problem. Encouraging an open and honest atmosphere without fear of reprisal will save a lot heartaches and headaches for the employee and employer alike. The biggest assets a business leader can bring to his or her employees are integrity, care and communication.

Miscommunication is a common occurrence. In my own company, the organization was split into various mini-company departments: Production and Assembly; Machining; Soldering and Fluxing; Contract Administration and Sales; Computer Information System; Accounting; Quotations; Purchasing; Quality Control; and Shipping & Receiving. For years, our policy was to have periodic individual meetings within each department but without any real structure. They served as an update of the current tasks for the department head's office, but too many times relevant information from other departments was not properly communicated or was forgotten. The atmosphere was a little too loose, despite the many good intentions. "Assumptionitis," or somehow assuming the other department knew the necessary information, crept into our business, resulting in mistakes and misunderstandings.

We needed to do something different. Why not involve others and hold scheduled weekly meetings for all department heads? We looked to our own in-house "advisors"— our key people—and held our own Advisory Team Meetings, or ATMs.

The ATMs, held early in the week for no longer than one hour, brought together our department supervisors. Each person had a role of an advisor so they could freely bring out issues for discussion and for brainstorming. They were encouraged to bring lists of the work that was in progress, goals for two weeks, plus ideas and concerns that needed to be addressed. Each department head shared the priorities, the orders being processed and unresolved problems. At times, someone would give an idea that would be of help to that particular department. More issues were resolved. Employee strengths also became more apparent as people responded to situations. Flexibility helped to deal with changes. A lot of direction and support came from within the meetings. The communication flow increased substantially, resulting in reduced mistakes and errors and greater reliable information and accuracy, as well as increased sales since shipments got out faster. Accomplishments were recognized. And we eliminated "assumptionitis."

Tips

Many companies rely on accurate internal communications to accomplish a given task. Each employee has her or his own role and an understanding of how it affects others. Involve as many people as possible so that the proper picture can be painted as accurately as possible. The following is a suggested format for establishing advisory team meetings:

- Develop a written agenda or list of items for discussion and review it ahead of time. Set a time limit for the meeting and for each participant to speak. Allow sufficient time for input and for creativity. Review ongoing work and set goals for the following week or two.

■ Encourage communication and employee participation by your own actions. There may be courses at a local community college or private training programs that may be able to help your workers become more self-reliant and capable of making decisions.

■ Many companies ask their employees for suggestions. To get the message across to employees that their input does matter, be sure to follow up on their ideas quickly. Do not put it off. It demonstrates that suggestions are taken seriously.

■ Formality can backfire. It is important not to make employee suggestions an elaborate form or require pages to be filled out. Just by talking about it at a one-on-one meeting or by having a group meeting, in an informal atmosphere with all those who have responded, shows support and consideration for any idea. Providing financial incentives or sharing of savings or revenue can produce excitement. If this is done, be sure it is communicated to all involved. Be creative.

Summary

Encouragement of ideas involves greater communication. It can open many doors within the company. Establish regular meetings to pursue suggestions and review ongoing practices. Do the hours invested in these meetings produce results? Keep notes and be responsive even if the suggestion is not adopted. How receptive are you to new ideas? Why not invite those with ideas over lunch at the golf links?

THE CREATIVE ONE
Thinking Out of the Box

9th HOLE: While your guest is taking a practice swing on the tee, you decide to take a few experimental swings with your driver to see if you can improve your play. You are trying to create better follow-through. Your guest is getting ready to hit and you finally stop swinging your club. You decide to check your golf bag for tees. Despite making a little noise, you continue to search, even as your guest is now ready to hit the ball. You don't stop since you believe that your guest does not hear the noise.

A. No harm is being done since the guest is not saying anything about the noises being made.

B. You know you should try stopping the noises but it does save a little time.

C. Have a little patience and wait.

Score (Par 4)
5: A is a bogey. Eventually, your movements will disrupt your guest. It does not matter if you were trying to be creative with your golf swing. At least you stopped swinging, but moving any clubs, balls, loose change, etc. must also end.

Would you like it if your guest was doing this while you were concentrating on hitting the ball? There are no excuses.

4: B is a par but it is not much better despite good intentions. Resist the temptation and be quiet. It is only for a few seconds.

3: C rates a birdie. It can be hard just to wait an extra second or two, but the little things do add up. Your guest will appreciate it. Why run the risk of making a lot noise and getting a look of dismay or worse?

Thinking Out of the Box

We all have ideas. Wherever I worked, from time to time I explored new product ideas or services that would eliminate a problem or provide a better solution. In my own company, we tried and tested new ways to improve production or processes and perhaps come up with a "million-dollar idea." Although we never had a formal suggestion box, we did have meetings on a quarterly basis with our employees regarding their work that included time to discuss matters that would further help the company. Ideas about eliminating or combining certain production or assembly operations resulted in improved process flow and generated ideas for more productive equipment. Do not overlook those within your own company, no matter what their role or job may be. A new insight or perspective may be lurking just around the corner.

At times, we would contact customers for their reaction to a new product idea. Questions were asked as to what future needs may be or what are their service or product limitations. We also wanted to confirm what we thought or see if we missed something. Otherwise, we may have invested a large amount of capital and time before realizing that someone else had the same idea. Investigate, do a patent search, search the Internet, and seek advice from a patent attorney. You can get so emotionally tied into the concept that you may overlook key aspects or problems. Keep an open mind and do not take constructive criticism personally. It is about business.

It is also important to have a signed confidential disclosure agreement before presenting a new idea for the first time to anyone or any company. This should not be overlooked, no matter how long you may have known the person or business.

Tips

When an idea strikes, do you follow a list of procedures to be sure all aspects are considered? For review:

- Put your idea into writing. List the various pluses and minuses. What problem are you trying to resolve? Where did the idea originate? Have you conducted a patent search? The United States Patent Office grants patents only when a completed application is filed and an official search is conducted. Visit this website for information: www.uspto.gov/web/offices/pac/doc/general/.

- Have you thoroughly searched the marketplace? Have you asked for other opinions? Have people sign a nondisclosure and confidentiality agreement regarding your idea.

- Seek opinions of others, such as key customers and suppliers. Be open to constructive criticism. Search out other services, products, companies or industries.

Listen to what is being said. It may trigger an even better idea before you spend significant funds.

■ Have you written an article, column or book? Are you protected? Do you know the copyright law? See http://lcweb.loc.gov/copyright/. A good resource on self-publishing is Dan Poynter's work called *The Self-Publishing Manual: How to Write, Print and Sell Your Own Book.*

■ Save articles on how others discovered new ideas and became successful, particularly those that inspire you.

Summary

Creativity is time well spent. Keep possibilities open. Schedule appropriate times for business-to-business golf. Play in tournaments, pro-ams, member-guest events at other courses, too. Accept invitations.

IN WRITING, PLEASE
A Paperless Society... Sort of

10th HOLE: At the start of each hole on the course you are playing, there is written information regarding the distance and a diagram of the hole to be played. Further down the hole, the sprinkler heads in the fairway list the remaining distance to the green. For example, after hitting a good drive off this hole, you were able to determine for your second shot, how many yards remained to the green by using the fairway yardage indicator. In this case, there are 135 yards to go. You proceed to hit the ball and it lands just short and to the right of the putting surface. The green is small. Using your pitching wedge, you attempt to hit the ball up high and have it stop near the pin. As you swing, you inadvertently pick up your head and the ball sails over the green. You are visibly upset and say a few things that are not particularly nice or within golf etiquette. You see that your guest is surprised by your anger. You should:

A. Apologize immediately and go right to the next shot.

B. Offer an apology, but wait until the hole is completed since your guest seems to have a temper also.

C. Your anger does not really matter since a club was not thrown.

Score (Par 4)

3: A rates a birdie since you dealt with the issue immediately.

4: B is a good par and helpful. Do apologize regardless of the personality of your guest. It is an opportunity to show that you care and that you are responsible for your actions.

5: C is a major bogey and an invitation for disaster despite the fact that your guest may not show it. Even if your guest had used profanity on a previous hole, do not feel it is acceptable. Your anger does matter.

A Paperless Society ... Sort of

What do you do after attending an industry seminar, trade show, or business meeting? Do you review your notes? Do you carefully consider major points that may generate an idea for your business or do you just forget about it?

I learned from experience to keep notes and to refer to my calendar each day. Writing, keeping notes and having an organized procedure have saved me much time and agony. It enables me to focus on the priorities.

In financial services, especially with insurance, a lot of information was requested as part of the application process. It was reviewed by the company's underwriting department. The policies that were issued normally required an explanation to help the client understand the clauses and conditions of coverage. I even had my own notes as reminders of helpful thoughts.

In the manufacturing business, we insisted that every production operation be put in writing, not only for the Production Department, but for ourselves. If a computer crashed, a manual copy of instructions could be quickly located. It provided peace of mind and enabled us to review our procedures, too. If a key employee were to leave suddenly, we were able to build from the information collected and train new people.

Quality control had a manual that documented our manufacturing, office, purchasing, engineering, drawings, returns, safety and other procedures. Any new changes required a revision. Input by the appropriate department was sought. Though it consumed time and resources, it improved our organization, generated confidence, and served as a reliable reference for company policies and procedures.

As an example, a number of manufacturing, service companies, and health care institutions have achieved, or are in the process of becoming ISO 9000 registered. ISO (International Organization of Standards) is a formal and highly visible document that puts into writing the company's practices and procedures. It helps with internal organization and responsibilities. It can be used as a sales tool for your customers. It shows that you have taken a major step in documenting your management system practices. Whether it is ISO or some other documented quality management system, it is a key guide to your everyday work and verifies what you say you do in writing.

Tips

Do you have your business processes documented? Is there a back-up, especially if a key employee leaves? How organized are your offices and how quickly can you find information? Consider the following:

What are your business processes and who is responsible? What are the strong and weak areas? Is it in writing? If a key person suddenly leaves your company, is the information leaving with the employee?

A quality management system documents many critical areas that companies rely on to do business. For example, contract administration, sales, purchasing, shipping, customer satisfaction and corrective actions are included. Though it requires much work, effort and documentation, ISO 9000 is a working system that helps a company with its processes, procedures and departmental responsibilities.

There is a major surge in paperwork in our computer age. Regardless of what you may read or hear about, the drive in high technology towards a "paperless" society—the Information Age—has brought both more information and more paper. If you need to get out from under the paper load in your own office or company, consider taking a one-day course or hiring an organizational consultant. A good place for information is the website www.thepapertiger.com.

Being organized helps save time. In Richard Koch's book, *The 80/20 Principle: The Secret of Achieving More with Less,* the author shows how the Pareto Principle (referencing economist Vilfredo Pareto) can work to our benefit. For example, it may hold true, as it generally did for me, that 20% of the clients represented 80% of business sales. In Koch's publication, the point is made that a business may be spending an extraordinary amount of time, perhaps as much as 80%, on areas that are only marginally profitable at best. Save time by being focused, organized and having things in writing. Do things that you're good at and that you enjoy.

If you are out of the office visiting clients or prospects often, use the waiting time efficiently by reading industry articles; keeping a note pad accessible by writing down thoughts or ideas that come to you; network with people while waiting in line; update your list of things to do.

Summary

One of the greatest time-savers is being organized. Put your priorities in writing and look at them each day. Keep small note pads handy especially in your car. Seek input from others within your own organization, or from a professional you respect. Keep notes on your basic fundamentals, especially when things are going well. This also applies when you are playing good golf. Keep good notes. When things are not going according to plan, you will have a ready reference for review that may provide you with a good idea by recalling a positive experience.

TAPPING INTO OTHER RESOURCES
Finding the Right Assistance

11th HOLE: You have learned that your guest is a golf committee member at the golf club to which he or she belongs. Both of you discuss what the committee is doing and agree that memberships in other golf associations offer an excellent opportunity to meet other people, share experiences and learn of other resources. During the conversation you realize you forgot the score your guest had from the last hole, which was played poorly. You decide to:

A. Wait until later to ask your guest's score.

B. Just fill in an approximate number and drop the subject.

C. Ask immediately even though your guest had a bad score.

Score (Par 5)

5: A is a par score if you do not wait more than one hole. But why wait? Are you embarrassed? Unless there is a good excuse, ask for the score when the next hole is finished so you can record both at the same time.

6: B is a bogey since it shows denial. It may be even more awkward to bring up the subject later on, especially if the guest is not playing well. Ask immediately. Also, make it a habit to record the score on each hole you complete before teeing off on the next hole. When recording scores, make sure that you are far enough away from the green and are not holding up play for the group behind you. This helps move play along in a timely manner and shows your guest that you are organized and courteous.

4: C is a birdie. This is best since it clarifies the situation and puts it behind you. It does not matter whether the score it a good one or not, just record it on the scorecard and proceed to the next hole.

Finding the Right Assistance

In my insurance experience there were two main types of customers: individuals and commercial accounts. In the manufacturing company, our customer base consisted of two types also: commercial and government. Federal government agencies required a lot of reporting. The people at these government buying offices were more than willing to work with us on expediting purchase requests, pricing history, quotation information, etc. A lot of companies may choose not to participate with government bids due to the many regulations that increase the cost of doing business. Much effort has been made over the last several years to reduce the large amount of specifications and regulations. Progress has been made. The government also outsources products and services to private companies, resulting in savings of time and cost.

Whether you are in the government or the commercial arena,

there are rules, regulations, guidelines and information resources to assist your efforts. It is very helpful to attend seminars, obtain the latest information, and network. For my business, we received government standards and specifications at a minimal charge.

The government is an excellent payer as long as you complete the appropriate forms and documents. We never had a check bounce! Once you have experienced working the system a few times, it becomes routine and part of your business climate.

It is important to maintain contact with each buying office. Visit their office and find the appropriate contact person. Review the steps that are necessary to process a bid or order. There are other resources that provide assistance such as websites or publications. Keep in mind, however, that the government is not a private business. There is a different relationship. You may not be able to contact the key decision-maker as you can in a private business. But keep your resources and information current, understand the process, and learn or know how decisions are made.

Tips

If you are currently doing business with the federal, state or regional government, or thinking about doing so, there are offices to help you, whether you are in services or manufacturing, self-employed or a consultant. For example, throughout the country, there exist regional Procurement Technical Assistance Corporations (PTAC). These offices help businesses obtain information on how the process fits together so you can seek business opportunities. It is a good resource for specifications, standards, and what is required to be able to bid on government contracts. The opportunities require your follow-through to make sure things are moving along. Some factors to consider:

■ Review the product or services classifications and keywords that best describe what your business offers. The Internet has several good starting points for working with the government. Search websites such as http://dodbusopps.com, the federal government information website www.business.gov. or http://nais.nasa.gov/fedproc/home.html.

■ PTACs can help walk you through the process of you selecting appropriate buying agencies. They can assist you in filling out information, but it is your responsibility to perform in accordance with the terms and conditions of any awarded project.

■ If you know of other companies that are doing government business, give them a call to see if you can meet and discuss the experience. Consider hiring an experienced private consultant who may be able to provide additional insight and other contacts.

Summary

There are many resources available from state, local and federal government agencies. For example, the state where your business is located has a website with a lot of good information that may lead to other areas (see Appendix for your state's website). This may give you ideas for your business and offer you a competitive edge. You may even be able to obtain some funding. Attend seminars, meetings, and workshops that may be sponsored at various locations —possibly at golf clubs.

ORGANIZATION MATTERS

Getting the Most from Your Business

12ᵗʰ HOLE: Your guest hits the golf ball into the rough, far off the fairway. Both of you search for the ball. You know the golf rule regarding the maximum amount of time that is allowed for looking for a ball—five minutes. Your guest appears to be unaware of it as time is running out and nothing has been said to stop the search. Should you:

    A. Consider mentioning the time limitation only if absolutely necessary.

    B. Do not say anything about it since this may annoy your guest.

    C. State the time factor when helping your guest look for the ball and be the one to implement it.

Score (Par 4)

4: A is par and may work out if the search is successful in a short period of time, such as two to three minutes. Do not wait much longer. Be sure you are helping the guest find the ball. Do not let your guest search for it alone. Please note—rules allow you to search for five minutes, but try not rush it. Why? When the person declares that he or she is giving up on the search, and drops another ball in play, it is this ball that becomes the only ball in play. A penalty for the lost ball is imposed even if the original one is found before the five minutes is up.

5: B is a bogey since you are feeling uncomfortable and simply do not want to confront the issue. Denial is bad and will only promote anxiety. If something is bothering you, say so in a diplomatic but firm way since you need to consider other players that may be waiting. The sooner it is said, the better, especially if you feel your guest has no idea of the time limit.

3: C scores a birdie. You are taking the initiative to expedite the search—not just for both of you, but out of time consideration for other golfers who may be waiting behind you.

Getting the Most from Your Business

Each company has a product or service for their customers. There is also a certain management method and style. The personalities involved provide the company with its uniqueness. But in every organization, the flow of a business organization is critical.

In order to make sense of it all, organizational charts are commonly developed. They should not be restrictive or lock anyone's talent up in a box. It may take some experimentation and practice, but with the proper approach and patience, talents and skills should define the work. In our business, we put the company chart in the front section of our quality control manual. We learned to keep revising it, depending upon our needs and the skill levels of our employees. It also helped us to properly delegate work to the appropriate person when necessary.

It was important in our company not to restrict a person's capabilities. We tried not to limit anyone's ability by virtue of their title on the company organizational chart. It was important for us to work in an atmosphere in which issues could be resolved openly. Many issues that arose were difficult but as long as we discussed the pluses and minuses of a given situation, encouraged thinking out of the box, and had the right tools to resolve the problem, our organization became quite flexible within a structured environment and enabled us to save time.

Some of the areas that were key for us were contract administration, production, and shipping and receiving. It was important to make sure that any special customer requirements and related correspondence, quantity and delivery were known. A system was established to have, at all times, copies of orders available for each of these three areas. It enabled a continuity of communication that produced results in less time. It may be worth the effort to have an outside third party, such as the MEP previously mentioned, or a consultant take a fresh and objective look at your business as needed.

Tips

The company organizational chart tells quite a story. It shows the many aspects of a business, but does not reflect intangibles such as risk, responsibility, and relationships. It also probably does not tell the business affiliations, unions, or associations as part of the entire process. Perhaps the chart should. Are you comfortable with how your business or company is organized, the flow of the work, and who is doing what? When was the last time you reviewed your company's organization? Here are some suggestions that may work for you:

■ Be sure to list the essential areas of your business and who reports to whom. There is no need to list actual individual names—just titles are sufficient and which area is linked to another. Create a chart that is representative for your way of doing business.

■ Review the flow of work to each area and make sure that what is on paper is indeed what actually happens during the business day. Does it work the way it should?

■ Decide what is important to you and to the company and how responsive each area is, especially in times of urgency or importance.

■ Update or revise the organizational chart every six months, at a minimum, to capture any changes made and the skills and abilities of your employees.

■ Time management is essential. Prioritize your work load and have a list of things to do ready for the next day.

Summary

How much time is wasted trying to figure out who is doing what? Are you aware of each person's skills? Do you delegate only a minimal amount of work to others? Can you delegate more work to qualified people to free up time? If so, be thankful and give credit where credit is due.

ON A ROLL

Targeting More High-Quality Customers

13th HOLE: Both you and your guest have played the last two holes very well. You have both had good momentum and are developing a good rapport. In fact, your guest is on a roll with a good score going. He or she is very upbeat and excited that this could be one of his or her best rounds of golf ever.

    A.   You are quite amazed that the guest is playing considerably lower than his or her handicap and feel that this is just too good to be true. You show little enthusiasm.

    B.   You are pleased the guest is having such a fine round and offer words of encouragement.

    C.   You feel it is best to ignore the excitement and just keep on playing.

Score (Par 4)

5: A is a bogey. Do not assume anything, especially if this is the first time you have ever played with the guest. This could be the opportunity you have been waiting for and a time for the guest to remember the day. Keep it positive and show enthusiasm. Business can wait and most likely will since golf is such a mentally absorbing game. Especially when playing well!

3: B is a birdie. It is so much easier to compliment and be supportive. Maximize the day with your encouragement and use this day as a positive reference on other occasions.

4: C is par. Why be neutral? Would you want to have support shown for a good shot, let alone a good round of golf? It does not mean that you are overly enthusiastic, but show genuine acknowledgment of the score and good shots made!

Targeting More High-Quality Customers

Business requires planning and preparation for future growth, direction to build a certain momentum, and getting on a good roll. Even though plenty of hard and dedicated work is needed and can be tedious and boring at times, accurate information and professional planning helps in looking ahead to develop an agenda for the future that will produce the desired results.

In financial services, it was important to know what management trends, developments and directions were taking place and how they could affect the clients. In our business, we engaged a professional team consisting of legal, accounting and industry experts to aid us. But the primary members were our key customers. We spent a great deal of time and effort learning which products our clients purchased and their reasons for purchasing our product. One hard fact stood out from among the rest. As mentioned in the Tenth Hole, approximately 80% of our sales came from just 20% of our customers. So we focused on their orders and why they bought from us. It gave us a more definite purpose, renewed our mission, and developed positive momentum since we knew what kind of customers we needed to target.

Our clients consisted of about two hundred companies throughout the United States and Canada. Certain companies purchased the same products time and time again, others varied, while others required special modifications. A lot of special orders came from businesses that were not among our top 20% clients. Many times the profit margins on these special orders were nonexistent.

We reviewed the gross margins, cost of goods sold, labor and overhead costs. We were surprised that even some of our key customer sales were not as profitable as we thought. With this information, we reviewed our operations, procedures, and the suppliers from whom we purchased. We improved our purchasing skills by asking for better quantity pricing and discount terms, consolidating orders, obtaining new or alternative suppliers, and spreading out certain deliveries for cash flow purposes. We also encouraged and implemented greater cross-training for our employees. This led to more diversity than ever before for our employees and helped to increase productivity. A greater and more reliable momentum built when our production people and our production supervisor became very creative and implemented many changes. We were on a roll. Shipments to our customers improved and complaints were minimized.

We also kept track of our quotations and how we fared on bids in comparison to our competitors, similar to my previous practice in tracking insurance quotations and contracts. Prior to any bid submission, we developed a simplified cost chart that listed our expenses per job, including raw materials, labor and overhead for each item.

Additionally, we maintained a unit sales chart for each product line. It was like looking at golf statistics (greens hit in regulations, birdies made, scoring average, etc.). This chart listed the amount of units sold each year by type and by total dollar sales. This information revealed year-by-year trends, something we did not recognize before we began to chart the data.

We also included our bank credit line availability, outstanding loans, monthly scheduled debt repayments, payroll and benefits expenses, insurance costs, etc. We then combined all of this information to show our gross margins at any given time.

Tips

Do you list your most important statistics? Can you readily assess your key costs? How are your sales listed—by type of units or services, volume or profitability? Who are your most profitable customers? Why do they place their business with you? Are there others that you can add to your list of key customers? Do you know what your top customers represent in overall sales to your business? A few tips:

- List your top 20% of customers first by gross sales, then by profitability. Is there a difference between the two listings? What are their industry classifications by SIC (Standard Industry Classification)? Is there a common thread?

- What about the balance of your clients, the ones outside your top 20%? How much time and effort are put into those and what are the results? Are there things in common, such as size or type of business? Are you just selling features and benefits and not listening to or understanding your client's real needs or problems for these orders?

■ How many lost orders or lost bids have you incurred during the past year or two? Have you contacted the buyer or decision-maker to see why your firm did not obtain the contract? Is there a pattern being developed that does not favor your company? If so, ask why. Treat the decision-maker to lunch and discuss.

■ Do you follow up or seek out other companies in the same geographical area as your key customers—the top twenty percent? When was the last time you did? Why did they buy from you? Have you been able to establish a pattern or trend?

Summary

Do you fully service your key customers? How many have you asked to a round of business-to-business golf?

14

THE COMPETITION STRIKES

Watch Out for Others

14th HOLE: Your guest is a very competitive golfer and plays serious golf. There have been brief conversations but nothing much about business up to this point. Now, it appears that the guest likes to talk and is doing more of it. You decide to:

A. Just let the guest do the talking.

B. Keep playing as you have been and do not pay much attention to your guest.

C. Try to capitalize on the situation by bringing up how competitive your business is.

Score (Par 3)

2: A is a birdie. Let the situation ride out and if the guest talks and talks, just listen.

3: B is a par. It is acceptable to keep playing your game, but you should pay attention to your guest and note any changes with the topics. Have patience.

4: C is a bogey and could be trouble. This is not the time to sell or bring up business. There is nothing to capitalize on even if you feel the person is taking golf too seriously, and talks mostly about the game.

Watch Out for Others

Competition was an ongoing factor with each business I worked in. It is important to know the competitive players in your industry or geographical region by the type of products or services they offer. To give yourself insight and a possible edge, it is a good idea to encourage your prospect or client to talk openly. You may be surprised how informative or knowledgeable he or she may be. Listen and understand his or her needs and experiences with competitors. You may place yourself in a position of helping the client to clearly understand the value of your product or service. Price, for example, may not be the number one issue.

In manufacturing, my company had a number of competitors. The market certainly had its key players. We constantly looked at our competition's quality, delivery, pricing and market share. We also looked for any new companies that entered the industry or for firms that may have merged or consolidated with industry players. We learned to be proactive rather than reactive to maintain or improve our marketplace position.

We also subscribed to a bid service that provided us with bid results. This listing was known as an "abstract" or a report of the companies that placed bids. It listed information such as price, terms of payment, delivery, and other relevant information such as any government set-aside provisions that were applicable. We attended trade shows, not just to find new suppliers but also to observe the competitors and industry trends. We subscribed to newspapers, newsletters and industry publications. We conducted Internet searches by using selected keywords. We reviewed other company websites. We asked customers why they purchased from us and performed customer satisfaction surveys.

In the insurance side of my career, the government was not our customer. Customers were the general public and businesses. To stay competitive, we compared our insurance products to the benefits provided and policy rates of our competition. But the key difference was service and responsiveness to the client. In manufacturing, service and quality were essential. Product pricing information was sometimes more difficult to obtain. Past procurement histories on selected items sometimes required going through the Freedom of Information Act office with a typical response time of about one or two months. Once obtained, this information kept us informed as to who was our competition on specific products and if there were any new entrants in our field.

Tips

How much time does your company invest in obtaining competitive information? What kind of business intelligence do you compile? When was the last time you actually obtained information on your competition? Consider the following:

■ Obtain literature, visit their website, or have a third party research information about your competitors for you. Directories such as Hoover's (www.hoovers.com), Dun & Bradstreet (www.dnb.com) or Thomas Register (www.thomasregister.com) may be helpful.

■ Search through Dun & Bradstreet credit information and in the Uniform Credit Code (UCC) filings for financial information.

- Talk to your customers about your industry and competitors. This can be tied into a customer satisfaction survey.

- Your salespeople can obtain information through their contacts. Help them be on the alert for competitive information from other salespeople in the industry.

- Service your clients first and foremost. Give your clients a reason to buy from you and to provide information regarding your competing firms.

- Look at competitors' ads in papers and business publications. Talk with individual leaders in your field of interest.

Summary

Search for information relevant for your business. Talk to others. Invite them for a round of golf, but be careful what you say or information you provide. Go to specialists and other contacts who have a lot of experience.

ROAD MAP
How to Get Where You Want to Go

15th HOLE: As your guest takes a practice swing or two, you begin to realize that a majority of your business-to-business golf rounds with clients and prospects have provided you with improved relationships and increased sales opportunities. You feel good about it. Now, with only four holes to go, you notice that both you and your guest are scoring about the same and you ask yourself—why not a little wager over these last four holes or something more serious? Is this appropriate?

A. A wager is acceptable but should be kept low and just for fun.

B. Ask if the guest would not mind a wager, perhaps a serious bet to keep things interesting.

C. It is probably best not to say anything since your guest has not brought up the subject.

Score (Par 4)
4: A is a par. If there is a wager, keep it low. Ask only if you feel confident that the guest may be interested or a hint was previously made. Otherwise, forget about it and just enjoy the game.

5: B scores a bogey since it may be difficult to recover if your guest says no. Why even consider making a serious bet? What does "serious" mean? Are things so boring that you feel this is necessary? Serious wagering is not a good idea at all to begin with and is certainly not encouraged under any circumstance, in business-to-business golf or otherwise.

3: C is a birdie and indicates that you are taking no chances. Just stay with the entertaining aspect of the round, sharpen up your game, and do your best to show your guest an enjoyable time.

How to Get Where You Want to Go

Many times we get caught up in everyday work. In my own business, the company's original mission took a different path, sometimes without realizing it, and we would hit some bumpy roads.

A plan of action was needed to provide better control. A business plan was the answer and it became our road map. It takes time to create a plan. It is dependent on good, reliable information such as sales (profitable or not), customer needs, trends, costs of goods, technology changes and so on. In addition, the manufacturing marketplace virtually mandated that we provide a rapid response to our customers, including any special order that required modifying a product.

In the insurance business, response time was also important. It was necessary to keep servicing your clients. New sources of business came from customers, other contacts, referrals and your own research. But the key was to keep making calls. The more calls made and the more customers talked to, the more business came your way. You could then develop a realistic business plan based on past successes and failures.

In the manufacturing business, referrals were rare. We had a strong client base and the overall market was not as open as the insurance market. We maintained good contact with our customers and were able to know what their purchasing requirements were or have an idea regarding possible up-coming buys during the next quarter or two. We reviewed our plan regularly. Our bank and accountant greatly encouraged it. It was an exercise not just for financial purposes, but it also kept us focused on our production needs. It led to greater understanding and knowledge of what our business was about. We reviewed each department, the positives as well as the negatives. We also reviewed our written procedures and compared them to what was actually being done. Differences were examined and corrective action was implemented. Once the corrections were made, we reviewed our goals and mission for at least one year. This provided direction and established a good road map. It also had the benefit of reducing excuses for not accomplishing tasks or assignments.

Tips

What is your business plan? Is it for one or two years or more? Does it involve each department?

- Review your company's mission. Has it changed from a short time ago? Are you capturing a good market share? If not, why not?

- Have you established a forecast of sales by year, month or quarter? What is it based on? Make sure your forecasts are in line with your business plan and overall strategy. You can help yourself by knowing your key customer profiles, for example, by industry classification. Why they are buying from you and how does your service or product satisfy their needs?

■ How do you measure results? Is it by sales only, or by product profitability, or as in the case with services, by project or billable hours? What is the percentage of sales from the top 20% of customers? What about the other 80%? Should some clients be dropped so you can refocus your time on the more productive clients?

■ Can you describe your particular market niche and estimate how many clients or prospects are there? Do you have significant competition? How much of the marketplace are they capturing? Can you calculate your sales success rate against your competition?

■ Do you need an infusion of cash to take your company to a higher level? There are a number of equity capital network opportunities. The United States Small Business Administration has an angel investor network that has information on possible investors for your business. The website is www.sba.gov/advo.

Summary

How does your competition obtain business? Do you know or can you measure results when you have entertained a guest on the golf course? Were you able to get your message across?

SUCCESSION PLANNING TO GO

Mastering Your Company's Future

16th HOLE: A few clouds appear with a threat of rain. A passing shower starts and ends within minutes. Though no lightening appears, the brief shower recalls the incident when a few professional golfers on the Professional Golf Association (PGA) tour were struck by lightning and nearly killed—a scary thought. Neither you nor your guest brought any rain gear and this could pose a real problem if the rain continues for a long period of time. To prevent this from occurring:

A. Always keep protective rain gear tucked away in your bag along with an umbrella.

B. A few towels should be good enough for you and your guest.

C. Assume you have appropriate rain gear and equipment and only check for it once in a while.

Score (Par 3)

2: A is the birdie. It eliminates doubt since the essentials are in your possession at all times.

3: B is a par but could still cause problems if you are at a far distance from the clubhouse. If there is any doubt before playing that there could be showers, take an umbrella, rain jacket and pants, and enough towels.

4: C indicates lack of preparedness and deserves a bogey. Assuming you have the needed items is heading for disappointment. Do not assume anything!

Mastering Your Company's Future

In banking, there is life insurance. If applying for credit, there is credit insurance. In estate and business planning there is business, life and disability insurance. In shipping products, there is insurance for shipping packaged goods.

In the manufacturing business, we often talked of what we would do if our business ever merged with another company or if it was sold. What we did not talk about much was what would happen to the business if one of the partners died or became disabled.

After a number of years without any insurance coverage, mainly because of cost and ignorance, and with the encouragement of our accounting and legal team, we decided to obtain life and disability insurance. The benefits outweighed the cost and we were insurable.

I have never regretted the fact that we finally decided to purchase insurance in case some tragic event occurred. We executed a buy-sell agreement for each partner. The premiums for the life insurance built up a cash value and enabled us to show a growing asset on the financial statements. The disability income plan, separate from the major medical health insurance, Social Security and worker's compensation programs, provided coverage for disability. The American Council of Life Insurance states that three out of every ten people become disabled for at least three months before age sixty-five and one out of five will be out for five years or more. This type of coverage can fill important income gaps if you do become disabled and are out of work for a lengthy period of time. Check with your financial team.

The insurance policies were good for us, the bank, our company, and, I am sure, for the insurance company! They also forced me to review my own personal coverage for my wife and family. We updated our wills with our attorney, who worked closely with our accountant and insurance people. But succession planning also involves non-insurance issues such as management succession, employee assignments and changes, benefits, reorganization and retirement, among other issues.

I would often ask myself due to the time, effort, and cost, if this was truly worth it. Without hesitation, the answer was a strong yes. It was an education, too.

A few years later, a customer approached us with an offer to purchase our company. Having a succession plan in place sent the message that we had taken the time and expense to provide a contingency plan in the event of unexpected events.

Tips
Is there a succession plan for your company? If not, discuss it with your attorney, accountant or insurance person, if you have not already. It is not only for protection. It is also helpful in

preserving your business. It should be reviewed periodically, at least once a year. Only a few states will assist in paying certain professional fees for succession planning. For example, New York has an Empire State Development program called the Ownership Transition Service (OTS). Statistics show that 70 percent of family-owned companies do not make it to the next generation. Why? Lack of a succession plan is a factor. Also, high estate taxes may force some companies to liquidate. Ask your professionals or the economic development office in your state for more information. Consider the following regarding succession planning:

- If you are currently without a succession plan, is there any reason why? Is it because of a family or business situation or is it difficult to talk about? Do you feel uncomfortable about the cost, or possibly being required to take an insurance physical? Do you not know where to start? Regardless of the reason, a succession plan is like a continuation of your company's business plan. Your business story cannot be properly completed without such a plan, since it ultimately affects the continuation of the business and each employee's job. A good place to start is by reviewing your assets and liabilities and listing your monetary goals and objectives.

- Confidentiality is a key part of the process as you discuss it with professionals. Do not hold back information that may affect any outcome.

- Visualize the end results by having a plan in place and envisioning how it could be a financial asset to your business and to you personally. This is also a good time to review your personal retirement goals and plans. Include verifying your estimated Social Security benefits by calling 800-772-1213 or go online to www.ssa.gov/mystatement. Under recent legislation, you should receive a summary of your estimated retirement benefits and disability income on an annual basis. Call if you have not received such a statement.

Summary

It is essential to preserve and protect what you have worked for and to ensure a cash flow in the event of a tragedy or ultimate retirement. Plan ahead. Have a golf round with an insurance representative, financial planner or professional consultant.

LINKS TO THE WORLD
Best of the Internet

17th HOLE: You are beginning to wonder how things are back at the office and whether you have received any e-mail, new work, quotations or phone messages. You initially resist the temptation to use your cell phone since you know that the workload has been delegated. After the next shot, you decide to call your office anyway. You become involved with a lengthy conversation and your guest is now waiting for you to finish your call. You feel:

A.   It was important to make the phone call.

B.   You should have called the office only if it was absolutely mandatory.

C.   You do not care how long the telephone call took and your guest should not mind.

Score (Par 4)
4: A scores par. Though it may have brought you up to date on matters at the office, ask yourself if it could have waited. Is it something you really had to do? Are you trying to impress the guest for some unknown reason? If so, and if you happen to be talking loud and the guest overhears a

discussion that appears to the guest to be minor, it will send a message that you are not putting your full effort into this business-to-business golf round.

3: B is a birdie. By resisting the temptation to call, you are giving your guest your undivided attention. If there are calls you truly need to make or may be expecting, be up front at the start of the business-to-business golf round so it will not come as a surprise.

5: C is a solid bogey as it implies that you obviously have other matters to discuss. It may give your guest a wrong impression that he or she may not be so important. And do take care how long any telephone call takes.

Best of the Internet

Many of us may associate the Internet with companies such as Amazon, America Online, Dell or Yahoo. You can order publications, music, or have a computer made to your specifications and shipped within hours. A lot of business activity on the Internet initially started with a business selling to the consumer, better known as business-to-consumer (B2C). But the bigger prize lies within businesses conducting transactions with other businesses over the Internet, known as business-to-business (B2B) or e-business (electronic business). What is this prize?

Take the establishment of TradeXchange by General Motors. The goal is to reduce the costs of doing business (overhead, labor, inventory, taxes—the Internet is still tax-free as of this writing) and ultimately free up working capital for other purposes by having purchase orders between companies conducted online.

According to studies, B2B e-commerce is expected to grow substantially and may be many times larger than the B2C market. A trend for many companies is to go to a specific industry website to order parts and services. Studies show that far less time is spent researching, faxing and phone calling. However, the lack of human intervention is a growing concern. It is important, despite the technological advancements, to forge business relationships with real conversations, good communication skills and meetings. Also, the federal and many state governments have substantially increased their use of the web, perhaps more than one may think. Not only do we have B2B, B2C, but also business to government, or B2G.

When our business obtained its first computer system we began slowly, then added more and more capacity. But, we needed help. In New York State, we were able to get assistance from Marist College, an advanced undergraduate school known for communications and computer science. We also received training from an Electronic Commerce Resource Center (ECRC) at Scranton College in Pennsylvania, one of several such centers in the country. Their home page (www.ecrc.uofs.edu) has a complete listing of the seventeen ECRCs throughout the country.

The growth of the Internet since the mid-nineties has been astounding, probably more so than any other media in history. Today, there are many business and golf websites that are highly informative and have many good links of their own to other sites. Those I have found quite useful are listed below. There are many others, but that is what you have to be careful about with the Internet. Watch out

99

for the amount of time you spend on it. There is so much out there on the Internet, I wish I could spend many more hours searching. Before I go searching on the world wide web, I ask myself where I am going, the reasons why, and then set a time limit.

We were able to learn about electronic commerce or business-to-business transactions relatively quickly, but not without mistakes and frightening moments. We considered it a major investment and learned a lot —learning never stops. Some of the key things to remember about electronic business are as follows:

- Be sure your website domain name reflects properly your corporate identity and what your company does. It may be helpful to register similar domain names, common misspellings, or other common names, too. Protect the name uniqueness and by claiming not just the .com, but also the .org and .net, too.

- Assuming you have a company website, update it weekly or at least monthly with at least some business news or announcements. Remember, the website is a marketing and information tool, but do not assume it will sell for you automatically. It needs constant review and attention for not just content, but also for technical aspects such as connections (dial-up or DSL or T1). Make sure your site is listed on all marketing and stationary pieces, press releases, ads, etc.

- How do people and companies find your website? Optimize your presence with keywords. Compile a list of about twenty to thirty relevant keywords for your business, paying particular attention to key phrases that you believe people need to use to find your website. Be specific and avoid "dead words" that are too generic, such as business, golf, free, the, Internet, etc. Listing in search engines takes time and many major search engines may charge fees. Search engines automatically visit other websites and create catalogs of web pages to their database. Directories are created by a human being and evaluated to see if there is a fit and if a site can be assigned to an appropriate category. Also, link your site to as many other appropriate sites as possible on a regular basis.

- Does your website conduct much electronic business directly with customers, business partners, suppliers, sales force, customer service representatives or others? Can you use any existing online software or services? Continuously keep in mind how secure your information is and who has access to it. There are many business-to-business electronic sites available. Take a look at full-service business-to-business application providers at www.i2.com or www.manugistics.com.

- How do you analyze your website information for visitors and users? There are websites that are very helpful such as www.webtrends.com and www.thecounter.com. Be sure your website is kept current and provide updates regularly.

Eventually, we became more productive and were able to lower overhead costs. This occurred by having spent less time in purchasing and accounting. Added time was used to develop our website as a marketing tool for reference with customers.

Whether you are in services or manufacturing, searching for good and reliable information is important. It is also important to keep track of your time. Make sure you create time for business-to-business golf opportunities to establish *golfships*. Do you delegate work to others and acknowledge those who help you? Be sure to give credit where credit is due.

Tips

The following list is provided to help you save time researching the Internet and to provide you with good information and links to maximize your time for business-to-business golf:

Selected golf websites:

www.usga.org – governing body of golf

www.pga.com – men's professional tour site

www.lpga.com – women's professional tour site

www.pgatour.com – information on the professional tours

www.thegolfchannel.com – television guide of golf

www.golf.com – golf news and information

www.golfcourse.com – guide to thousands of golf courses

www.golfdigest.com – commentary and information

www.golfonline.com – variety of golf subjects

Selected business websites:

www.suppliermarket.com – source for products

www.bizbuyer.com – bid requests

www.insweb.com – insurance information

www.toolkit.cch.com – business owner's toolkit

www.steel.com – information and links

www.hoovers.com – financial resource

www.ezgov.com – government information access

www.mediametrix.com – Internet and digital measurements and rankings

www.mep.nist.gov – information for business

www.infospace.com – news and resources

Summary

Use the Internet for gathering information about your customers, prospects, industry, competitors, resources, golf, and so on. It should be a regular part of your work plan. Obtain computer training to further develop your skills while navigating the Internet as needed whether from within your company or from an outside party to create more free time for business-to-business golf.

BUSINESS-TO-BUSINESS GOLF
Close That Deal!

18th HOLE: Though the round was seemingly enjoyable for you and your guest, you felt some tension during the round of business-to-business golf. What can you do to improve for the next time?

    A. Practice prior to the round as much as you can so that you release the tension you feel and can be ready to play.

    B. Realize that once you are out there on the links, it is best to relax and not worry about conducting business unless the client brings up the subject.

    C. Deny any tension you may feel about the round.

Score (Par 4)

4: A is the par score but watch out for over-practicing.

3: B is a birdie and shows that proper business-to-business golf is primary. You are there to entertain your guest, develop a relationship, have a good time and pay attention to the needs of your guest. Put yourself in your client's shoes. Ask yourself how you would expect to be treated.

5: C is bad news and ranks a bogey. Is the tension due to nervousness about the guest, your golf or both? If anything, review the information you have on the guest or company and talk it over with someone in your office. For the golf, practice a little bit a day or two before or go to a practice range.

Close That Deal!

At times, the pressure can be great playing business-to-business golf and it is not necessarily because of the golf score. It may be about business, how to build the relationship, what impressions your client or prospect is receiving from you and vice versa. You may question if it is worth the effort. I have learned that a round of business-to-business golf greatly helps to know the person you invited. Business may or may not actually be discussed, but it is important to develop good will and a public relations value. It may be that you and your guest will agree to meet another time, at any location, to discuss business. That's good.

Throughout the chapters in this book, there have been a number of golfing situations and business topics designed to help you play business-to-business golf at peak levels. As a summary, the following tips are meant to make your business-to-business golf a good experience and help you develop a good business relationship that will grow for you and eventually help close a deal:

Tips

- Do not bring up business unless you are asked.

- Try not to over-practice on the range just before playing your business-to-business golf round. You may wear yourself out or cause fatigue. Hit only about a dozen shots as a warm-up. If anything, chip and putt a few shots on the practice green, visit the pro shop, be sure the arrangements are set (such as reserving a golf car or caddy, food, fees, use of lockers, etc.).

■ Pay for the golf car, lunch and tips. Have enough cash for extras.

■ Know basic golf rules and etiquette. For example, do not stand in your guest's putting line. If asked about how a putt may break towards the hole, state your opinion, but then go away. Give suggestions and information up front on each hole regarding distance, hazards, and how to best play for position. Note any out-of-bounds stakes. Mention any local rules. Do not take excessive time to play. If there is any doubt who is furthest away, let your guest be the one to hit first. Do not be in a rush to play. Don't be a speed demon when driving the golf car, especially if conditions are wet or when going down a hill!

■ Do not hold up play! Remember do not take more than five minutes to find a ball. If your guest or group is slow, let the group behind you play through, or suggest that others are waiting and that it is necessary to move on.

■ Be honest at all times! If you mistakenly hit a wrong ball, move it, or lose it, say so right away, take the penalty and move on. Show you have integrity and lots of it.

- Keep the score for both you and your guest, and check periodically for accuracy.

- Do not give out free advice unless asked. Encourage the person asking for advice to practice the advice on a driving range instead of during play.

- Compliment your guest each time he or she hits a good shot.

- With each golf shot, keep a safe distance from your guest and be careful of shadows causing distractions, whether on the green, tee or fairway. It may cost you without a word being said.

- Voluntarily repair ball marks on the green. This is probably one of the most violated areas of the game. If there is any kind of embedded mark caused by the impact of a golf ball, whether it is your shot or not, repair it. Even repair your guest's mark as needed. It will be appreciated.

- Be careful of making noises with your club, bag, loose change, a ball, etc., especially prior to your guest's golf swing.

- Never lose your temper over a shot, score, waiting to play, etc., and don't even think about throwing any clubs. Watch your language, too.

- If in doubt, ask for your guest's score once the hole is completed and you are off the green (so as not to hold up any group behind you).

- Refrain from using your cell phone or Internet device during play. If you absolutely must, mention this to your guest before the golf round starts so it is not a surprise.

- Suggest a good golf book to your guest.

- Be sure to drive the golf car yourself or discuss splitting the driving time as needed; go slow and watch for bumps!

- Make mental notes where you leave your bag, golf car, etc. Be sure they are always off the green and at least twelve feet away.

- Dress in accordance with your club's rules and advise your guest in advance to bring other clothes, if needed, for dinner. Watch for overdressing as it may intimidate your guest. Plan ahead and advise your guest what is appropriate to wear for the day and other functions.

- If it is agreed to make a wager with your guest or with a foursome, keep it light. Just be yourself, have fun and do not worry who wins the bet!

- Golf brings out a person's character. You will observe your guest's character and they yours. Accept it for what it is.

- Have a golf rule book and a copy of the local rules of the club in your bag. Look them over a day or two before playing.

■ Play your own game and do not worry about the score or outcome. Let what happens, happen. Relax, enjoy yourself and let your friendly and helpful attitude do the talking.

■ If your guest had a great round of golf, make sure he or she receives compliments from you. Give your guest the scorecard to keep or make a duplicate if it is needed for any special event or tournament.

■ If you are having a meal before or after the golf round, be sure all is paid for up front and avoid having a check brought over to you. Get the best seat for your guest, too. If there is a choice on the menu, mention selections that are favorites or what the club is noted for. Have the guest order first. Once the ordering is complete and the round of golf has been talked about, talking business or setting a meeting date to discuss business may be appropriate.

■ Send a thank-you note to your guest.

■ Be thankful for having the health and ability to play the game.

■ And what about the golf game itself? Be as relaxed as possible and do not try to impress or intimidate your guest with your business knowledge or golf ability (even if you happen to be a low handicapper). Resist the temptation, especially before playing a business-to-business golf round, to read a lot of golf books or magazines. Just focus on how you would like to be treated if you were the invited guest, keep an honest score, make sure things are in order for the day, keep your head down and follow through!

Summary

How much time do you dedicate to business-to-business golf and what do you expect to accomplish? What lessons did you learn? Make a list of those people you would invite.

Scorecard

Hole	Par	Circle Your Answer			Your Score
1	4	a=5	b=3	c=4	
2	4	a=4	b=5	c=3	
3	3	a=3	b=4	c=2	
4	5	a=6	b=4	c=5	
5	4	a=3	b=4	c=5	
6	4	a=4	b=3	c=5	
7	3	a=3	b=2	c=4	
8	4	a=5	b=4	c=3	
9	4	a=5	b=4	c=3	
Out	35				
10	4	a=3	b=4	c=5	
11	5	a=5	b=6	c=4	
12	4	a=4	b=5	c=3	
13	4	a=5	b=3	c=4	
14	3	a=2	b=3	c=4	
15	4	a=4	b=5	c=3	
16	3	a=2	b=3	c=4	
17	4	a=4	b=3	c=5	
18	4	a=4	b=3	c=5	
In	35				
Par	70				

SCORING

At left is a scorecard with scores for each of the eighteen holes of business-to-business golf. Circle your answer and the numerical value for each hole played. Then review your answers to determine how you are swinging your way to business-to-business golf success.

Note:

- Best possible score is eighteen birdies or eighteen under par, or 52.

- Worst possible score is eighteen over par, or 88.

- Par score is 70.

Consider yourself an established business-to-business golfer with a score of 70 or less.

APPENDIX

REVIEW OF MAJOR TOPICS

The following is a review of the major business topics that have been discussed throughout this book. The topics are designed to help you continuously keep your company as competitive, productive and profitable as possible, forming a strong foundation for business-to-business golf.

- Keep your business mission and goals as realistic, workable and understandable as possible for every employee.

- Provide the appropriate equipment and technology. Know what kind of information is best for your company and customer base.

- Maintain a good flow of work in your business and take pride in your surroundings.

- Know your business strengths and weaknesses, especially of each department. Have an outside third-party consultant provide the objectivity needed and know what to expect.

- Observe your workforce in action and make sure skills and talents fit his or her roles. Offer training.

■ Know your customers and their true opinion about your business. Encourage continuous dialogue and communication to keep one step ahead of your competition.

■ Identify and recognize mistakes. Take appropriate corrective action and encourage regular internal communications and employee input. Encourage openness, honesty and integrity.

■ Be prepared for surprises and anticipate that what can go wrong, will go wrong. Have a plan of to react from a list of alternative options.

■ Be open to new ideas. Do not become attached to an idea that your bias becomes costly in time and money.

■ Make sure your business processes and practices are documented. Do not leave your business vulnerable if a key person suddenly leaves.

■ Leverage your situation by discovering and using other resources, especially those offered by the government.

■ Keep your company's organizational structure current and clear for all to understand and manage your time effectively and efficiently.

■ Develop momentum from good sales and customers. Know why your key customers do business with your firm.

■ Pursue good competitive information on a regular basis.

■ Maintain a business plan and review it at least annually. Measure results against the plan.

■ Life is full of surprises. Be prepared for certain events that could drastically affect your business, especially an unforeseen health issue to you.

■ Use the Internet, but be conscious of the time allocated before going online and what you want to accomplish. Use other resources and people who can maximize your time on the Internet and do not diminish the use of human interaction in conducting e-business.

■ Business-to-business golf helps develop good will, public relations, and the ability to know your guest as they get to know you in preparation for further business opportunities.

The goal is to maximize your business by keeping it focused on its mission, keeping priorities in order and enjoying an activity, such as golf, that can help your business.

BUSINESS PUBLICATIONS

Ansoff, Igor, McDonnell, Edward, Lindsey, Linda and Beach, Stephen. *Implanting Strategic Management*. 1993. Prentice Hall.

Carnegie, Dale. *How to Win Friends and Influence People*. 1994 re-issue. Pocket Books.

Collins, Michael P. *The Manufacturer's Guide to Business Marketing: How Small and Midsize Companies Can Increase Profits with Limited Resources*. 1995. Irwin Professional Publishing.

Cook, Marshall. *Time Management: Proven Techniques for Making the Most of Your Valuable Time*. 1998. Adams Media Corp.

Covey, Stephen R. *7 Habits of Highly Effective People: Powerful Lessons in Personal Change*. 1990. Fireside Paperback reprint edition.

Covello, Joseph and Hazelgren, Brian J. *Your First Business Plan: A Simple Question and Answer Format Designed to Help You Write Your Own Plan (3rd Edition)*. 1998. Sourcebooks Trade paperback.

Friedman, Jack. *Dictionary of Business Terms (Barron's Business Guides)*. 1994. Barron's Educational Series paperback 2nd edition.

Gerber, Michael E. *The E-Myth Manager: Why Management Doesn't Work—And What to Do About It.* 1998. Harperbusiness paperback.

Goldratt, Eliyahu M. and Cox, Jeff. *The Goal: A Process of Ongoing Improvement.* 1992. North River Press.

Grote, Dick. *The Complete Guide to Performance Appraisal.* 1996. Amacom.

Hartman, Amir. *Net Ready: Strategies for Success in the E-conomy.* 2000. McGraw-Hill.

Kaye, Beverly L. and Jordan-Evans, Sharon. *Love 'Em or Lose 'Em: Getting Good People to Stay.* 1999. Berrett-Koehler Publishers.

Leohr, James E. and McCormack, Mark. *Stress for Success.* 1998. Times Books paperback.

Nolan, John A. III. *Confidential: Uncover Your Competition's Top Business Secrets Legally and Quickly—And Protect Your Own.* 1999. Harperbusiness.

Porter, Michael. *Competitive Strategy: Techniques for Analyzing Industry and Competitors.* 1998. Free Press.

Sandler, David H. *You Can't Teach a Kid to Ride a Bike at a Seminar.* 1995. Penguin Group.

Slater, Robert. *Jack Welch and the GE Way: Management Insights and Leadership Secrets of the Legendary CEO.* 1998. McGraw-Hill.

Ziglar, Zig (reader) *Goals: Setting and Achieving Them on Schedule.* 2 Audio Cassettes. Abridged edition. 1995. Simon & Schuster (Audio).

GOLF PUBLICATIONS

Armour, Tommy. *How to Play Your Best Golf All the Time.* 1995. Simon & Schuster Paperback re-issue edition.

Campbell, Malcolm. *Ultimate Golf Techniques.* 1996. DK Publishing.

Elkington, Steve with Sampson, Curt. *Steve Elkington's Five Fundamentals of Golf.* 1998. Ballantine Books.

Feinstein, John. *A Good Walk Spoiled: Days and Nights on the PGA Tour.* 1996. Little Brown & Co..

Frost, Mark. *The Match: The Day the Game of Golf Changed Forever.* 2007. Hyperion.

Frost, Mark. *The Greatest Game Ever Played: The Movie Tie-in Edition.* 2005.

Hogan, Ben. *Ben Hogan's Five Lessons: The Modern Fundamentals of Golf.* 1989. Simon & Schuster.

Hurdzan, Michael J. *Golf Course Architecture Design, Construction & Restoration.* 1996. Sleeping Bear.

Leadbetter, David. *Positive Practice.* 1998. Harpercollins.

Palmer, Arnold with James Dodson. *A Golfer's Life*. 1999. Ballantine Books.

Penick, Harvey with Bud Shrake. *Harvey Penick's Little Red Book: Lessons and Teachings from a Lifetime in Golf*. 1992. Simon & Schuster.

Russell, Mark (Introduction), John Andrisani, Timothy W. Finchem. *Golf Rules Plain & Simple*. 1999. Harper Resource.

Sampson, Curt. *The Eternal Summer: Palmer, Nicklaus, Hogan in 1960: Golf's Golden Year*. 2000.

Woods, Tiger. *How I Play Golf*. 2001. Warner Books.

WEBSITE RESOURCES

Associations:
>   www.asaenet.org

Buyers for Excess Inventory:
>   www.tradeout.com

Business Directory:
>   http://businessdirectory.dowjones.com

Business Funding Directory:
>   www.businessfinance.com

City Information:
>   www.oag.com

Domain Name:
>   www.networksolutions.com

Electronic Business:
>   www.ebcentral.com
>   www.cio.com

Employee Benefits Research Institute:
>   www.ebri.org

Federal Electronic Commerce Program Office:
> http://ec.fed.gov

Federal Acquisition:
> http://msfcinfo.msfc.nasa.gov/fedproc

Financial
> www.investors.com
> www.wsj.com
> www.bloomberg.com
> www.financenter.com
> www.wallstreetcity.com

Golf:
> www.golfspan.com
> www.customgolf.com
> www.golfsearchengine.com
> www.freegolfadvice.com

Links to Industries:
> www.industrylink.com

Patent Searching:
> http://patent.womplex.ibm.com

Product Purchasing:
> www.rightquote.com
> www.bestquote.com
> www.iprocure.com
> www.ihsparts.com
> www.onvia.com
> www.commerceone.com

Publications and Reports:
> www.prgguide.com

Specialized Searches:
   http://search.cnet.com

Statistics:
   www.bea.doc.gov/bea/dn2.htm
   www.census.gov
   www.stat-usa.gov

Technology:
   www.techweb.com

Travel Warnings:
   http://travel.state.gov

Trends:
   www.businesstrendanalysts.com

U.S. Business Advisor:
   www.business.gov

Weather Reports:
   www.intellicast.com

Web Dictionaries:
   www.webwords.net

Zip Code Locator:
   www.usps.gov/ncsc

STATE WEBSITES

Each state has a lot of information on their website and include many resources for business development, financial assistance, procurement assistance, minority and women's opportunities, international trade, various publications and other information.

Alabama:	www.ado.state.al.us
Arizona:	www.state.az.us/ep
Arkansas:	www.state.ar.us
California:	www.commerce.ca.gov
Colorado:	www.state.co.us/gov_dir/obd/obd.htm
Connecticut:	www.cerc.com
Delaware:	www.state.de.us
Florida:	www.floridabusiness.com/
Georgia:	www.state.ga.us
Hawaii:	www.hawaii.gov/
Idaho:	www.idoc.state.id.us/ages/businesspage.html
Illinois:	www.state.il.us

Indiana:	www.ai.org/bdev/index.html
Iowa:	www.state.ia.us/government/ided
Kansas:	www.kansascommerce.com/
Kentucky:	www.state.ky.us/
Louisana:	www.state.la.us
Maine:	www.econdevmaine.com/
Maryland:	www.dbed.state.md.us/
Massachusetts:	www.magnet.state.ma.us/mobd
Michigan:	www.state.mi.us/
Minnesota:	www.state.mn.us/
Mississippi:	www.decd.state.ms.us
Missouri:	www.ecodev.state.mo.us
Montana:	www.state.mt.gov/
Nebraska:	www.ded.state.ne.us
Nevada:	www.state.nv.us.
New Hampshire:	www.state.nh.us/
New Jersey:	www.njeda.com/
New Mexico:	www.edd.state.nm.us
New York:	www.empire.state.ny.us/
North Carolina:	www.ncgov.com
North Dakota:	www.growingnd.com/
Ohio:	www.state.oh.us
Oklahoma:	www.odoc.state.ok.us
Oregon:	www.econ.state.or.us
Pennsylvania:	www.teampa.com/

Rhode Island:	www.riedc.com
South Carolina:	www.state.sc.us/commerce/
South Dakota:	www.state.sd.us/
Tennessee:	www.state.tn.us
Texas:	www.tded.state.tx.us
Utah:	www.state.ut.us
Vermont:	www.state.vt.us/
Virginia:	www.state.va.us/
Washington:	www.cted.wa.gov/
West Virginia:	www.wvdo.org
Wisconsin:	www.state.wi.us
Wyoming:	www.state.wy.us

Other

District of Columbia:	www.ci.washington.dc.us/
Puerto Rico:	www.prsbdc.org

GLOSSARY

Assumptionitis – A condition or state of assuming, in business or golf, that a situation will continue without much effort on anyone's part.

ATM – Advisory Team Meetings. In business, listening and understanding of issues by key employees. In golf, listening and understanding information or advice from your caddy, teammate or partner.

Birdie – A score on a golf hole that is one under par. You score a three on a par four.

Bogey – A score that is one over par. If you record a five on a par four, that is one over par, or bogey. Two shots over par, on a par four, or a score of six, is a double bogie.

Bunkers – Generally speaking, another term for sandtraps. However, grass bunkers are actually mounds of grass only (no sand) that surround a green, for example.

Business-to-Business Golf – Inviting your business client or prospect to a round of golf, giving you the opportunity to establish a stronger business relationship and foster good will. It is about business and enjoying a round golf. Your guest can be from your industry, a supplier, consumer, government representative, or even a competitor.

Cars, golf – The vehicles used on the course to carry the players and their golf clubs and equipment. Better known as golf carts. Carts are metal frames that hold a single golf bag and pulled by the player.

Fairway – The center section of each hole, between the tee and the green, with grass a little higher in length than that of the putting green but lower than the rough.

Golfship – Establishing a bond, rapport or relationship with the person with whom you are playing golf, regardless of whether if it is for business, enjoyment or competition.

Green – The very short grass on the course used for putting. Can also be used as a reference to the course as a whole.

Par – A score that matches par for the hole. If you took only three shots to play a par three hole, then you have scored a par. Your score is the same as the par for the hole, whether a three, four or five.

Rough – The tallest grass on the course. It can be cut to different heights. Rough is taller than the grass of the fairway.

Stroke Play – The recording of each golf shot (or stroke) for scoring purposes. **Match Play** is the recording of each hole won, lost or tied.

SELECTED GOLF RULES
(for Stroke Play)

The following are common golf situations that one should be aware of in order to achieve the maximium success at business-to-business golf:

■ Your guest asks you to mark your golf ball when on the putting green and to move it over two club head lengths of the putter. When it is your turn to putt, you mark your ball and play out. Two holes later, it dawned on you that you did not re-mark the ball back to its original spot—you forgot to include the two club head lengths. *Answer: This is a two stroke penalty. Add two strokes to your score.*

■ A ball is hit into a pond. There is an area marked where you can drop another golf ball. You stand straight, hold the ball at shoulder height, put your arm out and drop it. If the ball happens to touch you, your caddy or another player, it must be dropped again. If the ball goes beyond the allowed two-club lengths of where it finished up, how many times can you re-drop and what is the penalty?

Answer: You are allowed to try once more. If, after this second attempt, the ball is still outside of the allowed area, it can be placed as close to the spot as possible where you dropped the ball the second time.

■ A tee shot fades far off to the right into the woods, but you did see it hit the base of a tree and kick left. Just to be safe, you hit another shot, a provisional ball, as they call it, from the tee. At what point does a provisional ball come into play? *Answer: First, announce your intention of playing a provisional ball. Then, it can be played up to the area where the original ball was lost. If you cannot find the first ball, the provisional ball is now in play.*

• The ball lands in a sandtrap in front of the green. You are careful not to touch any sand as you address the ball. As you begin your backswing, you inadvertently brush some sand with your club as your start your golf swing. Is this a penalty? *Answer: Though unintentional, it is still a two stroke penalty.*

• Your tee shot is long but the fairway is tight with trees on both sides. Just off the fairway is deep rough and you are unable to find the golf ball. How much time do you have to find the ball before returning to the tee to hit again? *Answer: You are allowed five minutes to find the ball, even if someone declared it lost right after hitting it.*

• Your guest blasts out of a sandtrap and onto the fringe of the green about five feet short of the putting surface. Can your guest remove the sand and loose soil between the ball and the putting green? If not, is there a penalty? *Answer: If you do remove any loose soil that is not on the putting green, it is a two stroke penalty. Loose soil means twigs, leaves, branches, stones, worms and the like are allowed.*

- Your chip shot rolled up about thirty-five feet short of the flagstick. You ask your guest to hold the pin while putting from on the green. Your putt looks promising and goes towards the cup. Your guest just barely removes the pin as the ball drops in. If the ball had hit the pin, what is the penalty on your score? *Answer: It is a two shot penalty unless you were putting from off the green.*

- Your guest putts well but the ball stops on the very edge of the cup. How much time is allowed before taking the next stroke? *Answer: The golfer is allowed reasonable time to go to the ball plus another ten seconds. After that, if the ball has not dropped into the cup, it must be played.*

- At the next to the last hole, your guest runs out of golf balls and asks to borrow one from you. Without hesitation, you give your guest one. If this was an official tournament, could your guest borrow another ball from any player? *Answer: It is permitted as long as it does not unduly hold up play.*

- Your guest asks you if the location of the ball, whether on the fringe of the putting green, bunker, or green itself, has any bearing on the order of play. Does it matter? *Answer: It does not have any bearing. You should go by the player that is farthest away from the hole.*

Handicapping

Handicaps are an effort to level the playing field for all types of players. The United States Golf Association (USGA) plays a leading role in determining handicaps. The goal of the handicap figure is to officially state the number of strokes over par that you should take to play a full round of eighteen holes. If your handicap is 18, for example, and the course you play is a par 70, you are expected to shoot an 88 (88 minus 18 equals 70).

The USGA does not directly issue your handicap, or more appropriately, your handicap index. To obtain your legitimate handicap, you should join a club (public or private). The ten best scores you have made out of your last twenty rounds of golf and other pertinent information such as the golf course and course slope ratings will be factored into your handicap index. Any public or private course will have a computer that can calculate your handicap and issue you a handicap card for a nominal fee. Many local golf associations provide this service, too. Be sure to post all your scores.

If your guest does not have a handicap and you are not playing in a tournament, ask what his or her approximate average scores have been for ten rounds (or the number of rounds they have played) and use an average scoring figure to determine handicap. If you are playing in a tournament, be sure to check with the Golf Committee or with the local golf professional.

A net score is the result of the actual golf score minus the handicap. A gross score is a golf score without any handicap. In business-to-business golf, for most situations and particularly in the beginning of a business golf relationship, use the net score. Most tournaments or member-guest events, for example, will use a handicap format and you should produce an official handicap. If you and your guest are not playing in a tournament and your handicaps are the same, you may agree to play without handicap (or "scratch").

Course Notes

Each one of us understands the importance of keeping a golf course in as good shape as possible while playing. On the course, there should be plenty of signs on the links to remind us. But don't wait to see them; set the example. Following the items below will help you and others.

- Replace divots in fairways or wherever you see them.

- Repair impressed marks on the green from any shots you see.

- Rake sandtraps each time you use them and leave the rake outside of the trap area when finished smoothing the sand.

- Silence is golden whenever a swing is made. Refrain from moving things in your bag, golf car or golf cart.

- Record the score as soon as you are done with the hole, without holding up any players behind you.

INDEX

About the Author

Michael Andrew Smith has a diverse business career ranging from twelve years in the financial services field, including banking and insurance, to a partnership in a manufacturing business for twenty years. He has written articles on a variety of business topics and more than fifty newspaper columns on senior adult care issues. This is Mike's first book.

Mike works in the financial services field and is a speaker and author. He is involved with business owners, managers, sales people and decision-makers on a variety of projects. He has been playing golf for over thirty years and has won many amateur club tournaments and events. He is a member of the United States Golf Association.

Mike lives in upstate New York with his family where he continues to work, write, consult and play golf.

Order Form

Please send me ___ copies of *Business-to-Business Golf: How to Swing Your Way to Business Success.* Enclosed is $14.95 plus shipping. Call 1-914-850-6159 to inquire for pricing on quantities of 50 books and over.

Ship to (name) _____

Street address _____

City _____

State _____ Zip _____

Shipping & handling:
- Within United States: Add $2.00 per book.
- International: Add $3.00 per book.

New York State residents, please add 8.125% sales tax.

❑ I have enclosed a check for $_____. (Please make check payable to InfoPro Publishing.)

Please charge my: ❑ Visa ❑ MasterCard

Card number _____ Exp. _____

Name on card _____

Mail order to: InfoPro Publishing,
PO Box 4021, New Windsor NY 12553-0201

Fax orders: (845) 565-9204

Telephone orders: (845) 565-8763

E-mail orders: info@business2businessgolf.com

Website: www.business2businessgolf.com

Please send me FREE information on:
❑ Speaking ❑ Seminars/Workshops ❑ Consulting

Contact Us

We would like to hear from you regarding your round of business-to-business golf. Did you benefit from the information provided? Do you have any ideas that would help for future rounds of business-to-business golf? Please send your comments to:

InfoPro Publishing
PO Box 4201
New Windsor NY 12553-0201